The Wizard's Book of Puzzles

Margaret C. Edmiston
& Muriel Mandell

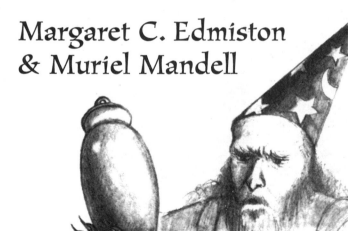

Sterling Publishing Co., Inc.
New York

Illustrations by Elise Chanowitz, Jack Williams & Jim Sharpe
Edited by Claire Bazinet

Library of Congress Cataloging-in-Publication Data Available

10 9 8 7 6 5 4 3 2 1

Published by Sterling Publishing Company, Inc.
387 Park Avenue South, New York, N.Y. 10016
© 2002 by Sterling Publishing Co., Inc.
The material in this book originally appeared in the following
Sterling publications: *Fantastic Book of Logic Puzzles*, *Merlin Book
of Logic Puzzles*, and *Fantastic Book of Math Puzzles*.
Distributed in Canada by Sterling Publishing
C/o Canadian Manda Group, One Atlantic Avenue, Suite 105
Toronto, Ontario, Canada M6K 3E7
Distributed in Great Britain and Europe by Chris Lloyd at Orca Book
Services, Stanley House, Fleets Lane, Poole BH15 3AJ, England.
Distributed in Australia by Capricorn Link (Australia) Pty. Ltd.
P.O. Box 704, Windsor, NSW 2756 Australia
Manufactured in the United States of America

Sterling ISBN 0-8069-0026-1

CONTENTS

Before You Begin

Puzzles are a time-honored fun-filled way of learning to reason logically, to develop thinking skills. They serve the same function for the mind as exercise does for the body. And they've been doing it for centuries.

Here are examples of many popular types of puzzles. All you need to solve most of these puzzles are paper and pencil or pen, a fresh mind, and a keen enjoyment of the challenge of a good puzzle. In a few instances, a knowledge of very simple algebra could save much trial-and-error time.

Should you get stuck, you'll find hints for some of the puzzles in the "Clues" section, where we may point out a tricky bit of language or reveal a particular approach to take. If the ins and outs of logic puzzles trip you up, read through the logic "helps" we've provided on pages 38 and 53.

Remember that, especially with logic puzzles, getting the correct answer isn't nearly as important as figuring out *how* to find it. So take your time with each puzzle and try to work it out. Use the hints and helps, if needed, to do it. Finally, check the detailed explanations provided at the back of the book to see if you got it right, or where you went wrong.

Now it's time to be off to a myriad of mythic kingdoms and medieval magic. Have a mind-bending trip!

MATCHING WITS

Not all matches are made in heaven, especially not the ones in this mythical kingdom. The matches here involve seven-league boots, potent magical potions, and specially-made weapons, and confront a motley crew of ogres, a court swordsmith, and a secretive wizard.

In these puzzles, you will find yourself converting words into mathematical symbols and formulas. You'll find them useful tools, particularly in some puzzles when the numbers multiply!

In the Dark

Planning to roam the countryside and prey upon its defenseless people, the ogre reached into his dark closet. There he had stored four six-league boots and eight seven-league boots. How many boots did he have to pull out of the closet to make sure he had a pair that matched?

Hint on page 82.
Solution on page 93.

Sword Play

The local king, determined to defend his kingdom from that wicked ogre, sent his two eldest sons to the court swordsmith.

The swordsmith kept a supply of special ogre-fighters (four daggers, three swords and two axes) locked in a chest. The two princes insisted on having the same kind of weapon.

How many weapons did the swordsmith have to take out of the chest to be sure he could meet the demands of the princes?

Hint on page 82.
Solution on page 94.

Anti-Ogre Potions

The king had his doubts about his sons' fighting skills, and so he sent his two eldest to the court magician for potions to help fight the ogre.

The magician kept his magic hidden, mindful of the danger of his potent potion falling into the wrong hands. In a secret but inconvenient compartment in his laboratory, he hoarded:

1. four ogre-fighters
2. three dragon-destroyers
3. two evil wizard-vanquishers

How many potions did he have to reach for in order to make sure that he could give an ogre-fighter to each of the king's two sons?

Hint on page 82.
Solution on page 125

Seven-League Boots

Meanwhile, back at the castle, the ogre found that the boots he had picked at random from his dark storeroom were all six-league boots. He threw them back. He needed seven-league boots so that he could cover more territory.

If in that dark storeroom he had four six-league boots and eight seven-league boots, how many boots did he have to pull out to make sure he had a pair of seven-league boots?

Hint on page 82.
Solution on page 93.

IN THE OGRE'S DUNGEON

The brainteasers in this section are classic problems in logic. After the first few puzzles that get you started, they all involve "if" statements. The conclusion depends on the "if" part being true.

Once you learn how to think them through, you may find these puzzles more fun than almost any other kind. Then, in "Genie Devilment," you can try dealing with several conditional statements—several "if's"—in a single puzzle, for an even greater challenge.

In the Forest

The king's only children, Abel, Benjamin and Paula, went into the forest with their friend, the elderly Sir Kay. They wanted to try their skill with their bows and arrows. Each of them started with same number of arrows. When all the arrows had been shot, it was discovered that:

1. Sir Kay brought down more game than Princess Paula.
2. Prince Benjamin captured more than Sir Kay.
3. Princess Paula's arrows went truer than Prince Abel's.

Who was the best marksman that day?

Hint on page 82.
Solution on page 94.

Captured!

Happy at the hunt, the king's children became careless and less watchful than usual. A passing ogre easily captured them and Sir Kay and took them back to his dungeon. He placed them in four cells in a row.

The cell in which Prince Abel was held prisoner was next to Prince Benjamin's. But Prince Abel was not next to Princess Paula. If Princess Paula's cell was not next to Sir Kay's, whose cell was?

Hint on page 82.
Solution on page 94.

The King's Heir

The ogre's prisoners spent a sleepless night in their dungeon cells wondering what fate awaited them. The next morning, the ogre approached the king's sons. "Which one of you is the king's heir?" he demanded.

"I'm Abel, the king's eldest son," said the black-haired prince.

"I'm Benjamin, the king's second son," said the one with red hair.

If at least one of them lied, who lied?

Hint on page 82.
Solution on page 95.

The Ogre's Boast

"I've devoured more than 100 humans," the ogre boasted.

"Surely, it must be fewer than 100," said Sir Kay.

"Well, I suppose it was at least one," said Abel.

If only one spoke the truth, how many humans did the ogre actually devour?

Hint on page 82.
Solution on page 97.

THE GENIE'S REVENGE

Did you know that our twentieth century computers use the number scale of the Australian aborigines and the African pygmies? Two, rather than ten, was probably the basis of our first number system. The solutions to some of the weight puzzles in this chapter hinge on this two scale, others on the three scale.

Weight puzzles first appeared in a collection published in France in the 1600s. They have been baffling puzzle fans ever since.

Hidden Gold

The clumsy apprentice of a wealthy Arabian merchant uncorked the jar in which a genie had been imprisoned for many years. Free at last, the genie looked about the Arab's shop to see what mischief he could make. He could, of course, have destroyed the merchant's shop or even killed the merchant, but he quickly realized that the merchant valued his money much more than his life!

Seizing the merchant's gold, he hid it at the bottom of a huge earthen olive jar. Then he brought in eight identical olive jars and placed three-pound weights in them. Last, he filled all the jars with olives and sealed them securely.

When the merchant became distraught at his loss, the genie revealed what he had done and agreed to give the merchant back his wealth if he could guess which jar held the gold. The genie would not let him open any of the jars. He could only weigh them. The catch? He could only use the scale three times.

The merchant owned a balance scale with pans on each side. How did he identify the jar with the gold?

Hint on page 83.
Solution on page 94.

Baskets and Baskets

The genie wasn't through with his tricks. In the merchant's warehouse were twelve sealed baskets of grain, one of which was fodder for pigs. The genie removed labels and rearranged the baskets so it was impossible to tell which contained pig fodder.

The merchant didn't discover the situation until a customer arrived to buy four baskets of grain. The customer was in a great hurry. If the pig fodder weighed a bit more than the other grain, how could the merchant, in one weighing, avoid the pig fodder and make sure he was selling fine grain?

Hint on page 83.
Solution on page 95.

Wanted—Pig Food

The merchant's next customer was a farmer whose storehouse was empty. He needed food for his animals. How many weighings did it take for the merchant to now find the basket of heavier fodder among the group of four baskets he had set aside?

Hint on page 83.
Solution on page 98.

Lead Weight

Thwarted by the merchant's ingenuity, the genie spirited away the merchant's scale and weights.

But the merchant made a scale by placing two empty baskets on either end of a long pole. Then he got a piece of lead weighing exactly 15 ounces.

He cut the bar into four pieces so that he could weigh objects from one to 15 ounces. What were the weights of the four pieces he cut?

Hint on page 83.
Solution on page 97.

Heavier Stakes

The merchant still had a problem weighing the heavier merchandise in his bazaar. He bought a 40-pound bar of lead. If he cut the bar into four pieces so that he could weigh items from one pound to 40 pounds, what would each piece have to weigh?

Hint on page 83.
Solution on page 98.

Weighty Matters

To weigh a 40-pound object with four weights—1, 3, 9, and 27 pounds—the merchant placed all of the weights on one side of the scale and the object on the other side.

But how did he weigh objects that weighed a) 5 pounds? b) 14 pounds? c) 27 pounds? d) 25 pounds?

Hint on page 83.
Solution on page 99.

Gold and Silver Coins

The genie was still making his way through the merchant's shop, messing up whatever he could. The merchant had 10 sacks, each containing ten coins. In one sack the coins were silver, in the others, gold. The genie slyly coated all the coins bright red and put them back in their original sacks.

The merchant knew that a gold coin weighed 10 grams and that a silver coin weighed a gram less.

If he used a regular scale, how could he determine in one weighing which sack was not gold?

Hint on page 83.
Solution on page 99.

GENIE DEVILMENT

We never seem to get quite enough information in puzzles that pose more than one "if" statement. As in life, we're only able to come to limited conclusions—and likely to mess up unless we're extremely careful about organizing and recording the information we do have.

Here, the genie has presented us with classic logic puzzles more challenging and complex than those in "In the Ogre's Dungeon." I hope you are ready for them.

The First Magic Number

Here are the conditions of the first number:
   A. If the first magic number was a multiple of 2, then it was a number from 50 through 59.
   B. If it was not a multiple of 3, then it was a number from 60 through 69.
   C. If the first magic number was not a multiple of 4, then it was a number from 70 through 79.
What was the first magic number?

Hint on page 83.
Solution on page 96.

The Second Magic Number

Here are the conditions of the second number:
   A. If the second magic number was a multiple of 6, then it was a number from 40 through 49.
   B. If it was not a multiple of 7, then it was a number from 60 through 69.
   C. If the second magic number was not a multiple of 8, then it was a number from 80 through 89.
What was the second magic number?

Hint on page 83.
Solution on page 99.

The Third Magic Number

Here are the conditions of the third number:
   A. If the third magic number was a multiple of 7, then it was a number from 30 through 39.
   B. If it was not a multiple of 9, then it was a number from 40 through 49.
   C. If the third magic number was not a multiple of 11, then it was a number from 60 through 69.
What was the third magic number?

Hint on page 83.
Solution on page 100.

MAGIC FORCES

Next, powerful forces and strong magic are at work. Look carefully at the changing pictures on the pages that follow. From the pattern of what has happened before, you'll be able to divine what will happen next—to predict the future!

The Wizard Waves a Wand

When a wizard waves his wand, mysterious things happen.

Before

After

Which of the following (A through D) happens next?

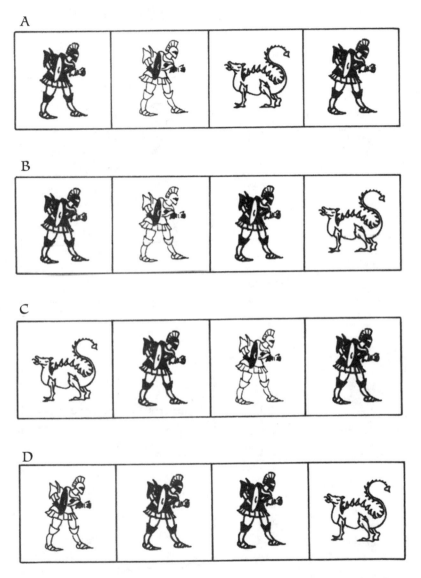

No hint.
Solution on page 100.

Knights and Their Weapons

Always preparing for combat, the knights practice with their weapons, like this:

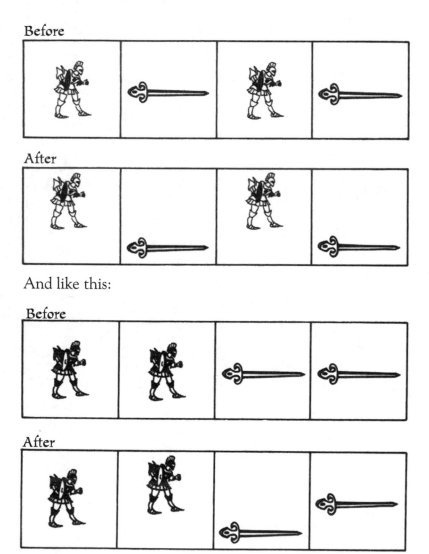

Before

After

And like this:

Before

After

This is the way things are done now:

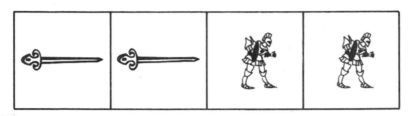

What happens next? Choose from A through D.

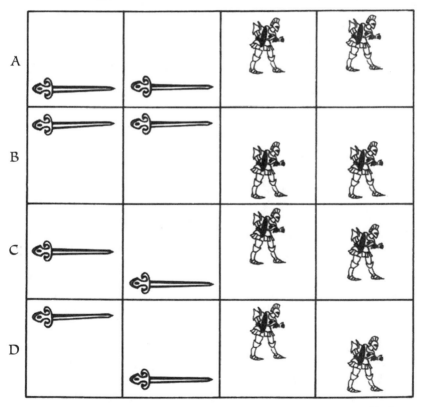

No hint.
Solution on page 122.

The Missing Swords

Decorating the walls of the Wizard Zorn's secret laboratory are sets of swords, each with different magic powers. One day, to his dismay, a rival sorcerer steals in and spirits away a set of Zorn's most potent weapons.

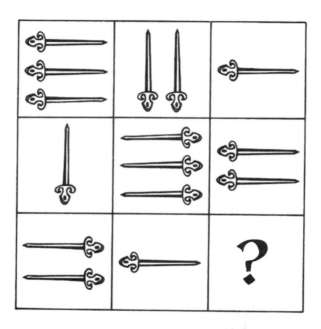

Which swords are missing?

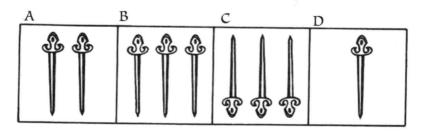

Solution on page 96.

The Genie and the Coins

How many coins were there in the sack the genie hid?

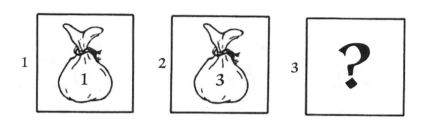

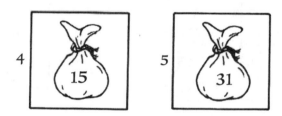

Choose one:

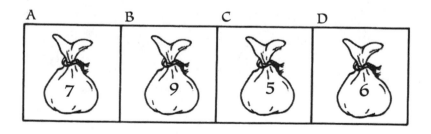

No hint.
Solution on page 109.

23

Genie Horseplay

What is the genie doing to the merchant's horses?

Before

After

Before

After

This is the way things are now:

What happens next? Choose from A through D.

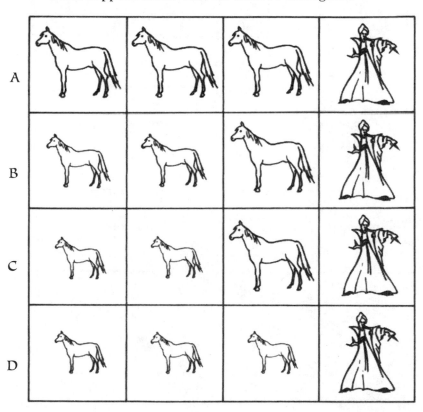

No hint.
Solution on page 114.

Genie Hijinks

To entertain himself, a genie sets things whirling.

What happens next? Choose from A through D.

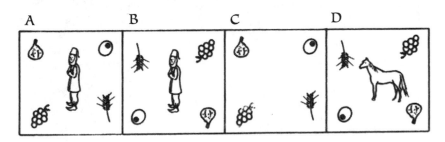

Solution on page 124.

Medieval Merry-Go-Round

A powerful wizard has created a spectacular illusion to entertain his guests. The images he has conjured up are spinning a circle.

What happens next?

Choose one:

No hint.

Solution on page 122.

MERLIN CHALLENGES YOUNG ARTHUR

Part of the grand and mystical legend of Merlin the Magician has him serving as the wise mentor and magical helper of the young king Arthur. One can easily believe that Merlin wanted Arthur to be a wise king, as well as a brave and noble one.

To improve the young king's reasoning powers, it is likely that Merlin challenged Arthur with the logic puzzles similar to those you will find in this section, involving knights, their squires, and other characters.

These traditional logic puzzles are the favorites of many people to this day.

The New Year's Eve Ball

On New Year's Eve, each of the first four knights to arrive at the castle at Camelot for the final ball of the year was mounted on a magnificent charger adorned in trappings that were the principal color of each knight's banner. In no particular order, these knights were Sir Pure, Sir Good, Sir Pious, and Sir Venerable. From the clues that follow, Arthur was to deduce the order of arrival of the four knights and the major color of each knight's trappings: blue, gold, purple, or white.

1. The four knights were Sir Pious, the knight who arrived second, the knight whose horse wore white trappings, and Sir Pure.
2. Sir Pious did not arrive first, and Sir Venerable was not the knight who arrived just before him.
3. Sir Venerable's steed didn't wear white trappings.
4. Sir Good arrived just before the knight whose horse wore blue trappings, who wasn't Sir Pious.
5. Sir Pure's charger did not wear purple trappings.

Hint on page 82.
Solution on page 100.

Who Won the Jousting Tournament?

Merlin challenged the young king with this logic puzzle as the two of them were sitting in the stands at the jousting field.

The problem was set forth as follows: at a recent jousting tournament in which a total of ten knights participated, the numbers 1 through 10 were assigned by lot to the knights. The tournament began with a contest between #1 and #2.

The winner of that contest went on to meet #3, and the winner of that second bout jousted against #4, and so forth. The last knight to remain unhorsed was the winner of the jousting tournament.

The task given to Arthur was to identify the participants in each of the nine matches, in order, and the winner of each, using the information given and the following additional clues.

1. Seven of the ten knights won no contests.
2. One contest was between #5 and #6.
3. One contest was between #7 and #9.
4. #2 did not joust against #4.

Hint on page 84.
Solution on page 101.

Name the Knights

Arthur may have been surprised when, just after he had solved the previous puzzle, Merlin asked him to deduce the names of the ten knights in the jousting contest. Merlin gave him the following clues, all of which pertain to the knights in puzzle #2. In alphabetical order, the knights were Sirs Bad, Black, Brave, Chaste, Glory, Good, Grand, Noble, Pure, and White.

1. Sir Pure's only contest was against Sir Black.
2. Sir Brave's only contest was against Sir Noble. Sir Brave wasn't #10.
3. Sir Good's single contest was four matches before that between Sir Noble and Sir Bad.
4. Sir Bad defeated Sir Grand.
5. Sir Chaste had the position number just before Sir White.
6. No two knights whose names begin with the letter B had consecutive position numbers.
7. Sir Glory and Sir Bad had consecutive numbers, in one order or the other.

Hint on page 84.
Solution on page 98.

The Rankings of the Squires

Arthur found this puzzle particularly fun to solve. His task: to determine how each of five judges, all knights, ranked each of five squires in terms of their overall promise as future knights.

The five judges were Sir Black, Sir Good, Sir Pure, Sir Noble, and Sir Wise. The five squires were Gort, Harl, Jol,

Kal, and Lok. In determining their rankings, each knight gave a score of 5 to the squire he considered the most promising, a score of 4 to the squire he considered the next-most-promising, and so on, so that he gave a score of 1 to that squire he considered least promising. Thus, each squire received five scores. These were totaled to determine the "most promising squire of the year."

The following additional facts were made known to Arthur:

1. Sir Black gave a higher ranking to Harl than Sir Good did.
2. Sir Noble's score for Harl was higher than any other score Harl received.
3. Sir Black rated Kal as Sir Good rated Lok.
4. Sir Pure's score for Kal was half Sir Noble's score for Harl.
5. Three knights, Black, Good, and one other, assigned their highest rating of 5 to Jol.
6. Sir Wise's score of 2 went to Harl; Sir Noble's score of 2 went to Kal.
7. Sir Pure and Sir Noble gave their 5's to the same squire.
8. Lok's total score was 21 points; Lok received a lower score from Sir Black than from any other judge.
9. One squire received no score higher than 3; his one score of 3 was given by Sir Pure.

Hint on page 84–85.
Solution on page 102–103.

Merlin and the Disguises

One day Merlin, Sir Good, Sir Kay, and two squires named
Alt and Maj were on a dangerous mission. It became desir-
able that each of the five should assume the guises of one of
the other four. As you can imagine, this was readily accomplished by the clever Merlin, and in such a way that no two
of the five assumed the guise of the same person.

Arthur's task was to figure out who was disguised as
whom. The clues that follow are sufficient.

1. Sir Good assumed the guise of the person who was disguised as Alt.
2. The person who assumed the guise of Sir Kay was portrayed by Merlin.
3. Alt assumed the guise of the person who was disguised
   as Merlin.

Hint on page 85.
Solution on page 101.

The Jousting Rankings

In this very challenging puzzle, Merlin gave Arthur a list of ten knights as follows, telling the young king that the list represented the rankings of the ten best jousters for the preceding year, #1 being the leading jouster, etc.

1.	Good	6.	Black
2.	Balter	7.	White
3.	Pure	8.	Brave
4.	Chaste	9.	Glory
5.	Grand	10.	Noble

"The rankings are different this year," said Merlin. "While the new list consists of the same ten knights as last year's list, none of the ten occupies the same position that he held the year before."

Arthur's challenge was to figure out this year's rankings of the ten knights based on the following facts:

1. The product of Sir Pure's ranking this year and his ranking last year is the same as the product of Sir Black's ranking this year and his ranking last year. Also, Sir Black's new ranking remains an even number.
2. The sum of Sir Chaste's ranking this year and his ranking last year is the same as the sum of Sir Glory's ranking this year and his ranking last year. Also, Sir Chaste's new ranking remains an even number.
3. The remaining six knights consisted of the following:
   (a) two who were consecutively ranked last year and remain so this year, having switched places in the rankings;
   (b) a third knight, who moved up one position;
   (c) a fourth knight, who moved down one position;
   (d) a fifth knight, who went from an odd-numbered position to an even-numbered one.

(e) a sixth knight who went from an odd-numbered position to a different odd-numbered position.
4. Sir Grand did not move to the #10 spot in this year's rankings.

Hint on page 85.
Solution on page 103–104.

The Pavilions of the Champions

The magnificent pavilions of the five knights judged to be the best jousters in Camelot were set up in a perfect circle on an elevated platform north of the field where on the morrow they would be obliged to meet the challenges of any and all knights who dared to brave their lances. (See the diagram that follows).

Before each pavilion, the emblem of the knight was

exhibited on his shield, hung for all to see, and beside each pavilion stood the squire selected to serve the knight during the tournament. Merlin's challenge to Arthur was to determine the name of the knight at each pavilion, that knight's emblem, and the name of the squire serving him on this occasion. The information given was as follows:

The Knights: Sir Brave, Sir Chaste, Sir Good, Sir Pure, & Sir White
The shield emblems: bear, dragon, oak tree, falcon, & lion
The squires: Altur, Bran, Col, Fel, & Hab

1. The pavilion of Col's knight was farther south than Sir Brave's.
2. Sir Brave's emblem was not the oak tree.
3. The pavilion marked "C" was the one where the knight's emblem was the bear.
4. Sir White's pavilion was east of only the pavilion where Altur was the squire and south of only the pavilion where the knight's emblem was the oak tree.
5. The pavilion of the knight served by Fel was west of only the pavilion where Bran was the squire and was not the pavilion where the emblem was the oak tree.
6. Sir Pure's pavilion was between that of the knights served by Bran and that of the knight whose emblem was a falcon.
7. The lion was not the emblem of Fel's knight.
8. Sir Good's pavilion was further north than that of the knight whose emblem was the dragon.
9. The pavilion of the knight whose emblem was the falcon was directly across from Sir Chaste's pavilion.

Hint on page 86.
Solution on page 106.

Deeds of Derring-Do

In the days before Arthur's reign, the land that was to become Camelot was on one occasion under the threat of a fire-breathing dragon that destroyed everything in its path, of a monstrous man-eating giant, of an evil knight who slew two of the bravest and noblest knights of the land, and of a Saxon spy who was cleverly gathering intelligence information for his own people.

Merlin chose four good and brave knights and said, "Go forth and find and slay these forces of destruction and evil. You will be protected by my powers."

The four knights, who were, in alphabetical order, Sir Bountiful, Sir Chivalrous, Sir Daring, and Sir Gallant, got on their mounts and set off. One went to the north, one to the south, one to the east, and one to the west, each to slay one of the dreadful and evil beings. Each took with him a favorite squire—they were, again in alphabetical order, Alain, Damon, Frey, and Golan. Arthur's task was to determine the nature of each knight's deed, his squire's name, the relative location of his foe, and also to deduce the order in which the four deeds were done.

The following information was given to the young king:

1. It was not Sir Chivalrous who slew the dragon.
2. The knight served by Frey, who was not Sir Bountiful, slew the giant; this was the first of the four deeds.
3. The deed of Sir Bountiful and that accomplished in a spot east of the future Camelot were consecutive deeds in one or the other order, and both were accomplished before Alain's knight went on his mission to kill the evil knight.
4. The deed of Sir Chivalrous, who was served by Golan, was the second of the four to be accomplished.

5. Damon's knight accomplished his deed in the north.
6. Sir Gallant's deed preceded that of the knight who met his challenge west of the future Camelot.

Hint on page 86.
Solution on page 105.

THE LOGIC OF DISJUNCTION AND CONJUNCTION

Solving some of these puzzles, similar to what Merlin faced, calls for an understanding of the logical concepts of disjunction and conjunction. For example, if I say, "I will go on vacation in June, or I will go on vacation in July," or, more simply, "I will go on vacation in June or July," you would take my statement to mean that I will go on vacation during *either* the month of June *or* the month of July, but not during *both* those months. However, should I be fortunate enough to go on vacation both in June and in July, you would still agree that my statement ("I will go on vacation in June or in July") was true. In logic, this inclusive use of "or" (disjunction) is universal. If P and Q are two statements, then: "P is true or Q is true" means that at least one, and possibly both, of P and Q are true.

We also need to agree on what is meant when we say that the statement "P is true or Q is true" is a *false* statement. Such a statement is false only when *both* statements, P *and* Q, are false. In the vacation example above, the statement is true *only* if I fail to go on a vacation during *both* June *and* July; otherwise, it's false.

As to the use of the word "and" (conjunction), the statement "P is true and Q is true," or more simply "P and Q are true," is a true statement *only* when *both* P and Q are true, but it is a false statement if *either* P is false or Q is false.

CHALLENGES TO THE SORCERER HIMSELF

To solve the kinds of puzzles in this section, you need to use the contradiction method. You "assume" that some fact is true, then see if the assumption leads to a contradiction (of a fact known to be true). In real life, we do this without even realizing it. If someone, for example, says, "All dogs are poodles," you know it's not true because you know of other dogs that are *not* poodles (collies, for example).

So, for these puzzles what you do is: 1) assume that a particular fact is true; 2) check the assumption against the facts you have been given, until; 3) you find a contradiction or; 4) you are satisfied there is no contradiction.

Knights, Normals, and Spies

When England was constantly under the threat of invasion, spies were sent into Arthur's land to gather secret information. Let us imagine that a spy always lied, a knight was always truthful, and all others were "normal people" who sometimes told the truth and sometimes lied.

Merlin was always on the alert to identify spies. Here are some of the situations he might have encountered.

Knights, Normals, and Spies I

Merlin encounters three individuals who are personally unknown to him. We will call them "A," "B," and "C." Merlin knows that each of the three is of a different type: one is a knight, one is a spy, one is a normal. The three make the following statements:

A. C is not a spy.
B. A is not a knight.
C. B is a knight.

Provide a classification of each of the three.

Hint on page 87.
Solution on page 106.

Knights, Normals, and Spies II

Merlin again encounters three individuals who are unknown to him. It is known that one is a knight, one a spy, and one a normal.

A. B is a normal and his statement is true.
B. I'm a normal.
C. B is a normal or his statement is false.

Provide a classification of A, B, and C.

Hint on page 87.
Solution on page 108.

Which One Is the Knight?

Once more Merlin encounters three individuals unknown to him. Each makes a statement. Merlin knows only that at least one of the three is a knight. Which one is definitely a knight? Can it be determined what the others are?

  A. B is a spy.
  B. A is a knight.
  C. Either A or B is telling the truth.

Hint on page 87.
Solution on page 95.

The Three Suspects

One of Merlin's apprentices reported an incident in which three men were tried for being spies. Said the apprentice, "The judge knew that at least one of the three was a spy and at least one of the three was a knight."

"What did the three say at their trial?" asked Merlin.

"I don't remember exactly," said the apprentice, "but I do know that, on the basis of what was said, the judge, who is known to be a superb logician, was able to determine that only one of the three was a spy and was able to identify him."

"What do you remember about what the suspects said?" asked Merlin impatiently.

"Well, I know that the second suspect said that what the first suspect said was false and that the third suspect said that the first suspect was a spy. I also remember that the first suspect either said he was a normal or said that he was a knight, but I can't remember which."

From this information, Merlin was able to figure out what the first suspect had said and also to determine which suspect was definitely a spy. Can you?

Hint on page 87.
Solution on page 107.

Liars and Days of the Week

In an unusual land visited by Merlin in his travels, some of the inhabitants lie on Mondays, Wednesdays, and Fridays and tell the truth on the other days of the week, while the rest lie on Tuesdays, Thursdays, and Saturdays and tell the truth on the other days of the week.

What Day of the Week Is It? I

A Monday-Wednesday-Friday liar says, "I told the truth yesterday."

Hint on page 87.
Solution on page 104.

What Day of the Week Is It? II

In the same strange land, two inhabitants are encountered: one we will call "A," the other "B." A is a Monday-Wednesday-Friday liar. B is a Tuesday-Thursday-Saturday liar. On what day of the week is it possible for A and B to make the following statements:

A. Yesterday was Sunday.
B. Tomorrow is Saturday.

Hint on page 87.
Solution on page 108.

What Day of the Week Is It? III

Two inhabitants of the same land are encountered. It is known that one is a Monday-Wednesday-Friday liar and the other a Tuesday-Thursday-Saturday liar. The two inhabitants make the following statements:

A. Yesterday I told the truth.
B. Yesterday was Monday.

What day of the week is it? Which type of liar is each of the two?

Hint on page 87–88.
Solution on page 110.

What Day of the Week Is It? Is It Fair or Raining?

In a still stranger land, the inhabitants are "truthers" or liars depending not only on the day of the week but also on whether the day is fair or rainy. Three inhabitants are met. It is known that A lies on fair Tuesdays, Thursdays, and Saturdays, and on rainy Mondays, Wednesdays and Fridays.

At all other times he tells the truth. On the other hand, both B and C lie on fair Mondays, Wednesdays, and Fridays and on rainy Tuesdays, Thursdays, and Saturdays. At all other times they tell the truth. A, B and C make the following statements:

A. It is raining and today is Tuesday.
B. It is fair or today is Tuesday.
C. It wasn't Wednesday yesterday and it won't be Wednesday tomorrow.

What day of the week is it? It is fair or is it raining?

Hint on page 88.
Solution on page 116.

The Land of Green Elves and Stolen Baked Goods

Merlin was called to the land of the green elves where an epidemic of petty stealing was taking place. It seemed that no elf wife dare put her freshly baked goods on the window sill to cool without running the risk of some mischievous, pesky elf making off with them.

Who Pilfered the Pies?

In the first case, three elves suspected of stealing two pies were brought before Merlin. It was known that one of the three was innocent and the other two had conspired to the theft. It was also known that, of the statements made by the three, exactly one was true—not necessarily the statement made by the innocent elf. The statements of the elves were as follows:

    Arn: I am innocent.
    Birn: Con is guilty.
    Con: Birn is guilty.

Merlin was able to identify one of the two thieves, but of the other two, he was unable to tell who was guilty and who was innocent.

Hint on page 88.
Solution on page 108.

Who Stole the Bread?

In the next case, one of the same three elves was known to have pilfered and eaten two loaves of bread all by himself. The three made statements, and it is known that the thief made a false statement. Merlin was able to use this information to identify the thief. The statement made by the three were:

    Arn: I stole the bread.
    Birn: Arn is not telling the truth.
    Con: Birn stole the bread.

Hint on page 88.
Solution on page 100.

The Missing Meat Pastries

In this case, the same three elves were suspects in the case of the missing meat pastries. It was known that exactly one of the three was guilty and that only one of the three made a true statement; it was not known whether the true statement was made by one of the two innocent elves or by the guilty elf.

The statements the three made were:

Arn: Either Birn is guilty or Con is guilty.

Birn: I am not guilty.

Con: Arn isn't guilty.

Hint on page 88.
Solution on page 110.

The Doughnut Raid

Two elves were known to have been accomplices in the daring raid on two dozen doughnuts. Four suspects were brought in: Arn, Birn, Con, and a fourth elf named Dob. In this case, the suspects' statements are not at issue. What was known was that the following were actual facts:
1. If Arn is guilty, so is Birn.
2. Either Birn or Con, or both, is innocent.
3. If Con is innocent, Dob is guilty.
4. Con and Dob don't get along, hence would not have been accomplices.

Hint on page 88.
Solution on page 111.

A Master Robbery

In this final case, the same four elves were suspects in the master robbery of two different windows on the same day. Four pies and two cakes were stolen and presumably eaten by the rascally thieves. The following statements were made by the four. It was known that two statements were true and two false, and that the two thieves are the ones who made the false statements. It was also known that the thieves rode horses in committing the theft. The statements made were as follows:

Arn: Con can ride.
Birn: Either Con is guilty or Dob is innocent.
Con: Dob is guilty.
Dob: Either Con is guilty or Arn is guilty.

Hint on page 88.
Solution on page 93.

MORE CHALLENGES
FOR YOUNG ARTHUR

Arthur happily solved all the logic puzzles and begged for more, but Merlin waved the boy off impatiently. But, on an afternoon not long afterwards, when the young king was bored with his regular studies and tired of practicing with sword and lance, the sorcerer decided it was time for some more tests of Arthur's reasoning abilities. With arms uplifted and hands turned palm upwards, Merlin mumbled a strange-sounding incantation and Arthur was enveloped in a cloud of smoke. When the smoke dissipated, Arthur found himself with Merlin in a deep wooded valley between hills.

"All of these hills contain caves," said Merlin. "Some of the caves are empty, but those that are not empty contain either a dragon or a princess. The princesses have been imprisoned by an evil witch. Any you can find will be freed."

A Princess or a Dragon? I

"This is a puzzle I gave a Saxon spy to solve," said Merlin, "with the understanding that if he made the wrong choice, he would face the fire of a dragon, whereas the right choice would merely land him in prison."

Arthur found himself trembling as Merlin explained, "Look up the hill before you. You will see two caves. One of the caves contains a princess, and the other contains a fire-breathing dragon. Each cave has a sign above its entrance. One sign is true; the other is false. Which cave would you choose? The Saxon spy was forced to enter the cave he chose."

When Arthur hesitated, Merlin added, "Make the wrong choice, Arthur, and I will save you nonetheless." Arthur breathed a sigh of relief and went on to make the right choice. Can you? The signs read as follows:

A | At least one of these two caves contains a dragon.

B | A dragon is in the other cave.

Hint on page 88.
Solution on page 107.

A Princess or a Dragon? II

Arthur found the preceding puzzle to be very easy, and teased Merlin, "My dear Merlin, can you not in your wisdom come up with something harder than that? Surely the Saxon prisoner is in jail and not eaten by a dragon."

"You are correct, Arthur," said Merlin, "and for that reason, I found it necessary with future spies to devise harder tasks." Merlin mumbled some strange words, waved his wand, and Arthur found himself on a hillside facing three caves labelled "A," "B," and "C." Each cave had a sign above its entrance.

"Try your hand at this puzzle," said Merlin. "The facts are these: one of these three caves contains a princess, one contains a dragon, and one is empty. Only the cave containing the princess has a true sign above it. You must figure out the contents of each cave."

Arthur found this puzzle to be much harder than he did the previous one.

A
Cave C
is empty.

B
The dragon is
in this cave.

C
The middle
cave is empty.

Hint on page 88.
Solution on page 124.

A Princess or a Dragon? III

Merlin mumbled an incantation, waved his wand, and Arthur and he ended up facing two caves on yet another hill. "This puzzle is somewhat different," said Merlin to Arthur. "There are two caves, each with a sign above it. The signs are either both true or both false. You are to determine what each cave contains. Each contains either a princess or a dragon."

The signs read as follows:

A
Either this cave contains
a dragon or the other
cave contains a princess.

B
The other cave
contains a princess.

Hint on page 88.
Solution on page 112.

A Princess or a Dragon? IV

Merlin whisked Arthur off by magic to a hill with four caves labelled "A," "B," "C," and "D." "In this last princess or dragon puzzle," said Merlin, "two of the four caves have signs with true statements and the other two have signs with false statements. Each of the two caves with true statements contains a princess, and each of the two with false statements contains a dragon, so that, of course, the two caves with princesses have signs with true statements, and the two caves with dragons have signs with false statements."

The signs on the caves read as follows:

A | The cave next to this one contains a dragon.

B | The cave labelled "C" does not contain a dragon.

C | One of the caves next to this one contains a dragon.

D | The cave next to this one contains a dragon.

Hint on page 89.
Solution on page 105.

The Land of Pink and Green Fairies

Having successfully solved all the "princess or dragon" puzzles, Arthur was magically transported to the land of pink and green fairies, all of whom are female. Merlin explained to Arthur, "Real pink fairies always tell the truth, and real green fairies always lie. However, it is within my power to change a pink fairy to a green fairy, or a green fairy to a pink fairy, or both. A pink fairy disguised as a green fairy still always tells the truth, while a green fairy disguised as a pink fairy still always lies."

Can a Fairy Say "I'm a Green Fairy?"

Arthur's first puzzle was to answer the question: Is it possible in this land of pink and green fairies, for any fairy to say "I'm really a green fairy"?

Hint on page 89.
Solution on page 104.

Pink or Green Fairy?

Arthur was introduced to two pink-looking fairies, "A" and "B," who made the following statements:

  A. B is a green fairy.

  B. I'm the same kind of fairy as A.

Arthur was to provide a classification of each fairy.

Hint on page 89.
Solution on page 113.

THE LOGIC OF "IF–THEN" STATEMENTS

Before trying to solve some of these puzzle, we need to know what it means when we say that an "if-then" statement is true or that such a statement is false.

    Suppose I say, "If I stay home tonight, I will watch TV." The "if" part of this statement is the first part "I stay home," and the "then" part is "I will watch TV." Now everyone will agree that, if I stay home and I have made a true statement, I must watch TV. Also, everyone will agree that if I stay home and *don't* watch TV, I have made a false statement. But what if I don't stay home?

    Suppose I visit a friend and we talk. Was my statement "If I stay home, I will watch TV" true or false? Logically speaking, the statement is considered true. But, suppose I visit a friend and we watch TV together, what then can we say about the truth or falsity of "If I stay home, I will watch TV"? Again, logically, the statement is true.

    So, in formal logic, whenever an "if" statement is false, an "if-then" statement is true, whether or not the "then" statement is true. (The statement, "If horses have two legs, then I'm a monkey's uncle," is said to be a true statement. Think: if horses had two legs, *maybe I would be a monkey's uncle*.) But if the "if" statement is true, the "if-then" statement is true only if the "then" statement is true.

Three Pink or Green Fairies

Arthur soon realized that the color in which a fairy appears was irrelevant to her true nature. He told this to Merlin with some relish, but the old sorcerer merely replied, "A fairy's appearance is relevant in this next puzzle. Here are three fairies. Each will make a statement. Provide a classification of each fairy and answer the question, 'Does A appear to be green fairy or a pink fairy?'"

    A. B is a pink fairy.

    B. If A is a pink fairy, then C is a green fairy.

    C. B is a green fairy or A is what she appears to be.

Hint on page 89.
Solution on page 107.

The Land of Yellow and Blue Fairies

In another fairyland, the fairies, again all female, are all either yellow or blue. However, Merlin has changed the fairies' appearances so that all are striped yellow and blue. Each fairy also carries a baton which is either a magic wand or an ordinary stick. Whether magic wand or stick, all the batons look the same. Any fairy who is carrying a magic wand always tells the truth, regardless of her true color (blue or yellow), but any fairy carrying an ordinary stick always lies, regardless of her true color.

Merlin, of course, explained all this to Arthur before he transported the young king to this strange land. Then he gave Arthur some more puzzles to solve.

Yellow or Blue? I

A yellow-and-blue-striped fairy made this statement. "Either I am a blue fairy and I have a magic wand, or I am a yellow fairy, and I have an ordinary stick." Arthur was to determine what kind of fairy she is.

Hint on page 89.
Solution on page 111.

Yellow or Blue, Magic Wand or Not? I

A yellow-and-blue-striped fairy says, "I am a blue fairy and I am carrying an ordinary stick."

Arthur was asked to decide what kind of fairy she is and to determine whether she is carrying a magic wand or an ordinary stick.

Hint on page 89.
Solution on page 109.

Yellow or Blue? II

Yet another yellow-and-blue-striped fairy stated, "If I have a magic wand, I am a yellow fairy."

Arthur was to determine what kind of fairy she is.

Hint on page 89.
Solution on page 114.

Yellow or Blue, Magic Wand or Not? II

Two yellow-and-blue-striped fairies spoke to Arthur. Merlin explained that one was really a yellow fairy, and the other really a blue fairy. The fairies made the following statements:

A. I am a blue fairy and I am carrying a magic wand.

B. I am a yellow fairy and I am carrying an ordinary stick.

It was Arthur's task to figure out what kind of fairy each was, and what kind of baton each carried. Can you?

Hint on page 89.
Solution on page 116.

CHALLENGES TO A WIZARD APPRENTICE

Merlin decided to challenge a prospective apprentice with a number of puzzles, including many having to do with the science of mathematics. (You may be happy to know that many of them can be handily solved without using algebra.)

Boots for the Ogres

In a hole in the ogre's lair are three black boots, three brown boots, and three white boots. If the ogre removes one boot at a time without looking at its color, how many must he remove in order to be certain of having pairs of boots in the same color for himself and his two ogre-ous sons? (Ogres have two left feet, hence do not need boots for the right foot that are different from boots for the left foot.)

Hint on page 89.
Solution on page 112.

Monster Heads/Monster Feet

In a land inhabited by monsters, some monsters have two heads each and three feet each, while the remaining monsters have three heads each and four feet each. In all there are 120 heads and 170 feet. How many of each type are there?

Hint on page 90.
Solution on page 109.

King Arthur Meets with King Balfour

King Arthur and four of his knights met with King Balfour and four of his knights. The ten warriors sat at a round table with Arthur and Balfour directly across from each other, and four knights between them on each side, as shown below. In how many ways could the seats have been occupied by the eight knights if none of Arthur's knights sat next to another of Arthur's knights or to Arthur himself?

Hint on page 90.
Solution on page 125.

Tending Horses

Squires Col and Aken are each in charge of a string of horses. Col takes care of twice as many mares as Aken, who takes care of four times as many stallions as mares, and two more than Col takes care of, which is two more than the number of mares he, Col, takes care of. How many mares and how many stallions does each take care of?

Hint on page 90.
Solution on page 115.

How Long Did Dob Walk?

Dob, a stonecutter, comes home from work each day by ferry. His wife, Alicia, leaves their cottage at the same time each day to make the trip by mule cart to the ferry dock, meeting Dob at the same time each day.

One day Dob finished work before the usual time and took an earlier ferry, arriving at the dock one hour earlier than usual. Not wanting to stand about idly for an hour, he immediately began walking towards his cottage. Not knowing that Dob had arrived early at the dock, Alicia set out at her usual time and drove at the usual speed. On the way to the ferry dock, she met Dob and picked him up. They arrived at their cottage ten minutes earlier than usual. How long did Dob walk (assume a constant rate of speed for Alicia)?

Hint on page 90.
Solution on page 113.

Magical Substance

Merlin showed his apprentice a bowl full of some gray-looking matter. "This is magical matter," said Merlin. "If I put a 'dash' of it into an empty bowl, it will double its amount each day and completely fill the bowl in four days." How full is the bowl (what fraction of it is full) at the end of the first day?

Hint on page 90.
Solution on page 118.

Crossing the River

Sir Good and Sir Pure need to cross a river with an ogre, a goose, and a bag of corn. Available is a rowboat which will hold two people, or one person plus either the ogre, the goose, or the bag of corn. The problem lies in the fact that: a knight must always be present to keep the goose from eating the corn; a knight must always be present to keep the ogre from eating the goose; Sir Good is afraid of the ogre and won't be in that monster's presence unless Sir Pure is also present. Only the knights can row. How can everyone and everything get across the river?

Hint on page 90.
Solution on page 114.

THE LAND OF PYMM

Welcome to Pymm, a land inhabited by humans, elves, dwarves, and even Minotaurs. Here, kings rule, the Knights of the Golden Sword are the bravest heroes of the land, and armies small and large fight off invaders. In Pymm, dragons and other strange creatures (such as repulsive, monstrous glubs) are familiar menaces, wizards wield powers of good or evil, and the common people (stoneworkers, millers, cart drivers, shopkeepers, and ferry operators) go about their lives finding amusement at fairs and joining in festivities presented at the castles of their local kings.

How Much Did Alaranthus Weigh?

Pymm has many dragons. A few years ago, one of these dragons, Alaranthus, though not fully grown, weighed 1000 pounds plus two-thirds of his own weight. How much did Alaranthus weigh?

No hint.
Solution on page 116.

Weighing a Pound of Flour

"I want exactly one pound of flour," said the customer to the miller.

"Sorry," said the miller. "My scales are faulty. One arm is longer than the other."

"Do you have some lead pellets and a one-pound weight?" asked the customer.

The miller provided these things and the customer was able to weigh a pound of flour.

How did she do it?

No hint.
Solution on page 111.

Rings for the Princesses

There are a number of kings in Pymm, each with his own base of power and his own castle. One of these, King Firnal, had a box containing three gold rings. He wanted to divide the rings among his three daughters so that each received a ring, but one ring remained in the box. How could he do this?

No hint.
Solution on page 120.

Two Riders

A knight on horseback left Belft to ride to Dalch at the same time another knight left Dalch on horseback to ride to Belft along the same road. The first knight traveled 30 miles per hour and the second traveled 28 miles per hour. How far apart were the two riders one hour before they met?

No hint.
Solution on page 121.

A Lame Horse

A knight had ridden one-third the total distance of his trip when his horse became lame. He finished the journey on foot, spending twenty times as long walking as he had spent riding. How many times faster was his riding speed than his walking speed?

No hint.
Solution on page 108.

Jousting Tournament Number

Each of eleven competitors in a jousting tournament was given a number between 1 and 11. Sir Bale's son asked his father, "What is your number in the tournament, father?"

Sir Bale replied, "If the number of numbers less than mine is multiplied by the number of numbers greater than mine, the answer is the same as it would be if my number were two more than it is."

What is Sir Bale's number?

No hint.
Solution on page 121.

Inspecting the Troops

An officer on horseback rides slowly down a line of sixty mounted troops placed 10 feet apart. Beginning with the first man, the officer takes 29 seconds to reach the thirtieth man. At that rate, how long will it take him to reach the sixtieth (last) man?

No hint.
Solution on page 121.

The Human Population of South Pymm

One-third, one-fourth, one-fifth, and one-seventh of the human population of North Pymm, which has fewer than five hundred human inhabitants, are all whole numbers, and their sum is exactly the human population of South Pymm. What is the human population of South Pymm?

No hint.
Solution on page 120.

Measuring Two Gallons of Cider

"I want 2 gallons of cider for me and my pals," said Mongo to the shop owner.

The shop owner, who only sold cider from a huge barrel, replied, "I have a 3-gallon container and a 4-gallon container. Will you use one of those and guess at the amount?"

"I don't need to guess," said Mongo. "I can measure exactly 2 gallons using the containers you have."

How can Mongo do this?

No hint.
Solution on page 120.

WIZARDS, DRAGONS, & OTHER MONSTERS

Chased by a Glub

Pymm is inhabited by an unknown number of hideous monsters known throughout the land as glubs. Glubs live underground but can rapidly burrow to the surface if they smell a human, one of their favorite treats. Phipos was 5 feet away from a glub when he saw the fat, swollen monster advancing toward him. Phipos knew that he and the glub ran at the same rate and walked at the same rate (which was, of course, slower than their running rate), but Phipos also knew that the glub could spray him with an irritating fluid from almost 5 feet away. So he immediately began to run toward the safety of a fort several miles in the distance. At the same instant, the glub started chasing after Phipos.

Curiously, Phipos reached safety by first running half the time it took him to cover the distance to the fort, then walking half the time. The glub, which ran the first half of the distance to the fort and walked the other half, was never closer to Phipos than the original 5 feet. Can you explain this?

No hint.
Solution on page 110.

How Far Apart Were the Dragons?

The dragons Argothel and Bargothel like to get together for fiery conversations. They live some distance apart, each in his own cave. One day Argothel left home to visit Bargothel at exactly the same time that Bargothel left home to visit Argothel. The day being most agreeable, both dragons decided to proceed at a rather leisurely rate, for dragons. So, rather than fly, they walked. Argothel walked at a constant rate of 24 miles per hour and Bargothel at a constant rate of 36 miles per hour.

How far apart were they 5 minutes before they met?

No hint.
Solution on page 117.

The Farmer and the Hobgoblin

A farmer was at work clearing a rocky field for planting when an ugly hobgoblin approached him. The hobgoblin promised the farmer great wealth if he followed these instructions:

"Pick up a stone and carry it to the other side of the field. Leave the stone there and pick up another stone and drop it on this side of the field. Continue doing this, and each

time you cross the field and return, I will double the number of coins you have. However, because I don't want you to be overly rich, you must pay me sixteen coins each time after I have doubled your money."

The farmer, thinking only of the doubling of his money, readily accepted. Even after giving sixteen coins to the hobgoblin following his first crossing, he did not take the time to figure out what would happen if he continued with the hobgoblin's bidding.

After four crossings, the farmer was not only too tired to move, but he also had to give the hobgoblin his last sixteen coins. The farmer's pockets were empty and the hobgoblin went away laughing.

How much money did the farmer start with?

No hint.
Solution on page 115.

Wizard Rankings

Every Saturday at Pymm's End, a peninsula at the tip of southwest Pymm, there is a ranking of Pymm's End's six resident wizards. The rankings are based on the wizards' feats of magic for the previous six days. The highest ranking is 1 and the lowest is 6.

The rankings published on the Saturday before last listed Alchemerion highest because a spell had imprisoned an evil dragon inside an iceberg. Others listed were: 2. Bogara, 3. Chameleoner, 4. Deviner, 5. Elvira, and 6. Fortuna.

In last Saturday's rankings, each wizard was ranked in a different position from that of the previous Saturday. The following facts are known:

1. Bogara's change in ranking was the greatest of the six.
2. The product of Deviner's rankings for the two weeks was the same as the product of Fortuna's ranking for the two weeks.

What were the new rankings?

Hint on page 90.
Solution on page 124.

Did the Dragon Catch Pryor?

The dragon Wivere smelled half-elf Pryor at the same time that Pryor, who had been hunting in the forest, noticed smoke and fire rising from the direction of the dragon's mountain cave. Pryor realized the dragon was active and might try to catch him. Knowing that Wivere was afraid of water, he began to run toward the seashore. Wivere smelled Pryor but hesitated for 6 seconds before he began to run after the half-elf. The dragon ran because his wings were underdeveloped, compared to his ancestors' larger ones.

Wivere was 5 miles directly north of Pryor when Pryor began to run toward the sea 2 miles directly to his south. Pryor, who could run much faster than a human, ran at a rate of 20 miles per hour over the 2-mile distance.

Wivere's speed, however, was not constant. He ran the first mile at a rate of 20 mph, the second mile at a rate of 40 mph, the third at a rate of 80 mph, the fourth at a rate of 160 mph, and so forth—doubling his speed after running each mile. Did Pryor make it to the safety of the sea?

No hint.
Solution on page 125.

Minotaur Fighters

Three Minotaur leaders lent each other fighters from their armies. First, Logi lent Magnus and Nepo as many fighters as each already had. Later, Magnus lent Logi and Nepo as many fighters as each already had. Still later, Nepo lent Logi and Magnus as many fighters as each already had. Each leader then had forty-eight fighters. How many fighters did each have originally?

No hint.
Solution on page 124.

Human vs. Minotaur

A human warrior must fight seven competitors with his lance. Six of the seven are humans, and one is a huge Minotaur with a fierce reputation. The warrior is certain he will lose the battle with the Minotaur. He is about to end his life quickly by submitting to the Minotaur's lance, when the Minotaur issues this challenge.

"Arrange us seven competitors in a circle," he says. "Choose a competitor from this circle and, moving clockwise and counting that competitor as the first position, count to the seventh warrior and fight him. From there, assuming you win the contest, count seven more places clockwise. Continue in this way until you reach my place on the circle. If you manage to defeat all the others before your turn comes to fight me, I will spare your life."

How can the human warrior make sure the Minotaur is his seventh competitor?

No hint.
Solution on page 121.

EVERYDAY LIFE IN PYMM

At times when they were not being interfered with by the doings of wizards and sundry monsters, the people of Pymm went on with their daily lives—eating, building, travelling here and there. In doing so, they often found themselves faced with puzzles to figure out. Here are some of them. Isn't it strange that so much of it concerns mathematics?

How Many Cakes?

A banquet was given to celebrate a truce in East Pymm that put an end to clashes between humans and elves. Citizens from all races of East Pymm—humans, elves, dwarves, and half-elves—came together at the banquet.

After a huge dinner, sweet cakes were served for dessert. The first four beings at the banquet table emptied the first plate of cakes. (Luckily the castle cook had made enough sweet cakes for everyone to eat.) Heartnik, a human, took one-fourth of the cakes on the plate. Scowler, a dwarf, took one-third of the remaining cakes. Then Goodin, an elf, helped himself to half of the cakes left. Finally, Loglob, a half-elf, ate six cakes—all that were left on the plate.

How many cakes were on the plate in the beginning, and how many did each being take?

No hint.
Solution on page 113.

To the King's Castle

All the villagers in the realm of King Arthur were invited to a Christmas gala held at the king's castle. Alf and his wife, Beryl, left their cottage at 11 A.M. that morning and traveled by ox cart to the castle. At 11:30, an eager and impatient Beryl asked Alf, who was driving at a fast pace, "How far have we gone, dear?"

Alf replied, "Three times as far as the distance from here to the inn, where I will stop and have some nourishment."

The couple stopped at the inn for food and departed at 1 P.M. to continue their journey. Having overeaten, Alf became sleepy and drove much slower than before their stop at the inn. Afraid of being late, Beryl asked her husband, at 2:00 P.M., exactly 2 miles from the point where she had asked her first question. "Do we have much farther to go, Alf?"

Alf mumbled, "Three times as far as we have come since leaving the inn." Beryl then demanded that she take over the driving, to which a sleepy Alf readily agreed. The couple finally arrived at the castle at 3:30 in the afternoon. Despite the long journey, both thoroughly enjoyed all the festivities. What was the distance from the couple's cottage to the castle?

Hint on page 91.
Solution on page 122.

Building a Bridge

The dwarves Dobbit and Mobbit are building a bridge over a narrow stream. Dobbit can do the job alone in 30 hours; Mobbit can do the job alone in 45 hours. Dobbit worked on the project alone for 5 hours before Mobbit joined him. The two then finished the job together.

How long did it take the two to finish the job that Dobbit had started alone?

Hint on page 91.
Solution on page 114.

What Time Does the Wagon Driver Leave His Hut?

Once a week a wagon driver leaves his hut and drives his oxen to the river dock to pick up supplies for his town. At 4:05 P.M., one-fifth of the way to the dock, he passes the smithy. At 4:15 P.M., one-third of the way, he passes the miller's hut. At what time does he leave his home? At what time does he reach the dock?

Hint on page 91.
Solution on page 118.

Meeting the Stone Cutter

Every morning, a cart driver leaves the stone quarry to drive to the ferry landing, where he picks up an arriving stone cutter. The driver arrives at the landing at 6:00 A.M. and takes the stone cutter back to the quarry.

One morning, the stone cutter woke up before his usual time, took an early ferry, and, once across the river, began walking to the quarry. The cart driver left the quarry at his usual time and met the stone cutter along the road to the ferry landing. He picked up the stone cutter and took him the rest of the way to the quarry. The stone cutter arrived 20 minutes earlier than usual. At what time did the cart driver meet the stone cutter?

Hint on page 91.
Solution on page 119.

How Early Was the Barge?

Every day a cart is sent from a village to meet a barge at the river dock. One day the barge arrived early, and the cargo normally picked up by the cart was immediately sent toward the village by horse. The cart driver left the village at the usual time and met the rider along the way, after the rider had traveled for 8 minutes. The rider handed the load to the cart driver, who went back to his village, arriving home 24 minutes earlier than usual.

How many minutes early was the barge?

No hint.
Solution on page 119.

How Many Handshakes?

Fifteen knights were invited to a sumptuous meal at the castle in Belmar. Before sitting down, each of the fifteen knights shook hands with each of the other knights.

How many handshakes occurred?

No hint.
Solution on page 120.

How Many Schlockels?

Altus says to Bott, "Can you figure out how many schlockels I have in my pockets?" He then gives Bott three clues:

1. If the number of schlockels I have in my pockets is a multiple of 5, it is a number between 1 and 19.
2. If the number of schlockels I have is not a multiple of 8, it is a number between 20 and 29.
3. If the number of schlockels I have is not a multiple of 10, it is a number between 30 and 39.

How many schlockels does Altus have in his pockets?

No hint.
Solution on page 121.

A Round-Table Arrangement

The brothers Bob, Cob, Hob, Lob, Rob, and Tob always take the same seat at their round dinner table. The following diagram indicates their seating. The following is known:

1. Lob's seat is separated from Bob's seat by exactly one of the other brothers.
2. Hob's seat number differs from Cob's and Lob's, positively or negatively, by 2 and 5 in one order or the other.
3. Cob's number is 1 larger than Rob's number.
4. Bob's number is either 1 larger or 1 smaller than Tob's number. Which brother sits in which seat?

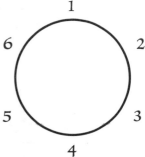

No hint.
Solution on page 117.

Which Coin Is Lighter?

Peppi, Bogara the Wizard's newest apprentice, groaned as he told elder apprentice Welch of the puzzle Bogara gave him.

"I've got fifty coins here. Fifty! Can you believe that they all weigh the same, except for one that's a tiny bit lighter than the other forty-nine. And I've got to find the lighter coin in four weighings on our balance scale. How in the world can I do that?"

Patting Peppi on the back, Welch told him that, indeed, the problem could be solved with a maximum of four weighings. Explain how this can be done.

Hint on page 91.
Solution on page 123.

The Sons of Blythe

Noblewoman Blythe said to noblewoman Alexis, "I have three sons. They are all less than 10 years in age, and the product of the ages of the two youngest equals the age of the one who, in years, has the greatest age. How old are they?"

"I can't find their ages from that information," said Alexis.

Blythe added, "My final clue is that the sum of their ages is a prime number." How old are Blythe's sons?

No hint.
Solution on page 119.

The Daughters of Alexis

After she had figured out the ages of Blythe's sons, Alexis herself, who has three daughters, asked Blythe to attempt to figure out their ages. "Your first clue is that the sum of their ages is 11," said Alexis.

"That is not enough information," replied Blythe.

"The product of their ages is either 16 years less or 16 years more than your age," added Alexis.

"Still not enough," said Blythe after careful thought.

"The daughter whose age, in years, is the greatest is learning to play chess," said Alexis.

Blythe was then immediately able to determine the ages of Alexis's three daughters. What are their ages?

Hint on page 91.
Solution on page 120.

How Far From Castleton to Devil's Peak?

A horseman left Castleton and rode toward Devil's Peak at the same time that a second horseman left Devil's Peak and rode toward Castleton using the same route. The two met for the first time at the point on the route that is four miles from Castleton.

The horsemen continued riding on to their destinations, then turned and rode back toward home at the same rate. Again they met, this time two miles from Devil's Peak.

Assuming both riders traveled at a constant speed, what is the distance between Castleton and Devil's Peak and what was the relative speed of the two riders?

Hint on page 91.
Solution on page 118.

How Did the Archers Cross the River?

A company of archers had to cross a river that had no bridge across it and was too deep to ford. They had just about given up on finding a way to do this when one of them saw two children on the river in a small rowboat. The boat was large enough to hold the two children or one archer, but was too small to hold two archers, or even one child and one archer. How did the archers get across the river?

No hint.
Solution on page 119.

How Can Everyone Cross the River?

A half-elf, an elf, a human, and a dwarf have to cross a river from the town of Ak to the town of Tok. They have a boat that will hold any two of the four, but no more.

Long-standing animosities exist between certain of these four beings, which make it undesirable for certain ones of the four to be together as pairs. While the half-elf gets along with the other three beings, the elf dislikes the human. The human dislikes the dwarf. The elf and the dwarf like and respect each other. How can the four beings cross the river if only the half-elf does the rowing, and no uncongenial pairs are together alone?

No hint.
Solution on page 114.

Feeding the Horses

Distal had enough hay and corn to feed his six horses for only 30 more days of the harsh winter, not for the remaining 75 days before spring arrived. On the seventh day, before feeding time, Distal sold four of his horses. Will he be able to feed his remaining two horses for the rest of the winter?

No hint.
Solution on page 109.

In the Dark

Don't be confused by the number of boots. There were just two *types*.

Sword Play

Ignore the number of weapons. Focus on the number of *types*.

Anti-Ogre Potions

The kind of potion the princes get is important since they are bent on fighting an ogre, not a dragon or a wizard.

Seven-League Boots

Refer back to the last puzzle, "Anti-Ogre Potions," above.

In the Forest

Take one statement at a time and make the comparisons.

Captured!

Draw the cells and the people in them so no statement is contradictory.

The King's Heir

Consider the possible true-false combinations:

	1	2	3	4
Black Hair	T	T	F	F
Red Hair	T	F	T	F

The Ogre's Boast

Which statements are not possible? Which statements contradict one another? Use the following "truth table" to organize the possibilities:

	A	B	C	D	E	F	G	H
Ogre	T	T	T	T	F	F	F	F
Kay	T	T	F	F	T	T	F	F
Abel	T	F	F	T	T	F	T	F

Hidden Gold

Divide the jars into groups of three.

Baskets and Baskets

Divide the baskets into groups of four.

Wanted—Pig Food

Consider how to divide the four baskets in order to weigh them.

Lead Weight

The solution lies in using the binary system, the scale of two, rather than a decimal system.

Heavier Stakes

Instead of using either the decimal system or the binary system, use a base of three. And remember, weights can be placed in the pan on either side of the scale.

Weighty Matters

When you place a weight on the same pan of the scale as the object you are weighing, you subtract that weight from the total of the weights on the pan on the other side.

Gold and Silver Coins

Line up the sacks of coins and number them from 1 to 10.

Magic Numbers (First, Second & Third)

For each of the magic numbers, make a chart involving all the possible numbers, such as the following:

50	51	52	53	54	55	56	57	58	59
60	61	62	63	64	65	66	67	68	69
70	71	72	73	74	75	76	77	78	79

Cross out those numbers that contradict any of the statements.

The New Year's Eve Ball

Make up a chart, using rows and columns, and enter into it the facts from clue 1 to obtain the following, in which one line is used for each knight.

	Knights	Order of Arrival	Color
1.	Pious		
2.		2nd	
3.			white
4.	Pure		

Use the other clues to finish filling in the chart.

Who Won the Jousting Tournament?

Keep in mind that every time there was a contest there was a winner and a loser. Try to determine which knights definitely won no contests and which did win one or more contests. Clues 2, 3, and 4 will determine the numbers of the three knights who, by clue 1, won one or more contests. Then use the rules by which the tournament was conducted to determine the opponents in each contest and the results of their meeting. (Special hint: from clue 3, #8 must not have won any bouts.)

Name the Knights

Make a list of the numbers of the knights—#1 through #10, leaving a line for each number—and fill in the names as you determine them. Certain clues will tell you the names of the three knights who won a contest—actually we know one of them won two contests, a second won three, and the third won four. So you can begin by writing their names down on lines 1, 5, and 7. When you determine which one of the three names belongs on each line, cross out the other two names. (Special hint: clue 3 is a key clue.)

The Rankings of the Squires

Make a chart as follows:

	Black	Good	Pure	Noble	Wise	Total
Gort						
Harl						
Jol						
Kal						
Lok						

Fill in all scores given directly in the clues, such as the scores of 5 given to Jol by Sir Black and Sir Good. As you determine other scores, enter them into the chart. Remember that in each column you should end up with one each of the numbers 1, 2, 3, 4, and 5.

Merlin and the Disguises

Make a chart and put in it the information from clues 1 and 3 as follows:

	Person's Name	Person's Disguise
1.	Sir Good	Person who was disguised as Alt
2.	Person who was disguised as Alt	Alt
3.	Alt	Person who was disguised as Merlin
4.	Person who was disguised as Merlin	Merlin
5.		

First, determine who was disguised as Merlin. By clue 3 that person wasn't Alt. Assume it was Sir Good. Do you find a contradiction? Assume it was Sir Kay. Do you find a contradiction?

The Jousting Rankings

To solve this puzzle it will be helpful to make up a simple chart like this:

	Last Year	This Year
1.	Good	
2.	Balter	
3.	Pure	
4.	Chaste	
5.	Grand	
6.	Black	
7.	White	
8.	Brave	
9.	Glory	
10.	Noble	

As you proceed to solve the puzzle, you will be trying out a number of different possibilities.

The Pavilions of the Champions

Make up a chart as follows:

	Knight's Name	Emblem	Squire's Name
A			
B			
C			
D			
E			

Begin with clue 3, and then use clue 4. Fill in the chart as you solve the puzzle.

Deeds of Derring-Do

Make up a chart like the one here, with a line for each knight, and fill in the information as you solve the puzzle. Beginning with clue 4, you obtain the following:

Knight's Name	Deed	Squire's Name	Location	Order
Bountiful				
Chivalrous		Golan		2nd
Daring				
Gallant				

Special hint: Clues 4 and 3 together identify Sir Chivalrous, Alain's knight, and Sir Bountiful as three separate knights and tell you the location of Sir Chivalrous's deed.

Knights, Normals, and Spies I & II

The way to do these puzzles is is to make a chart of all the possible combinations. Then, for each combination, look for any contradiction. If the puzzle has a valid solution, only one combination will satisfy all the given facts. The possible combinations are shown in the following chart:

Knight	A	A	B	B	C	C
Spy	B	C	A	C	A	B
Normal	C	B	C	A	B	A

Which One Is the Knight?

Start with C's statement.

The Three Suspects

Consider the four possibilities for A.
   A said he was a knight and he was a knight
   A said he was a knight and he was not a knight
   A said he was a normal and he was a normal
   A said he was a normal and he was not a normal
   Which one of the above satisfies the given facts?

What Day of the Week Is It? I

Make a list of the days of the week. Write down beside each day whether the person lies or tells the truth on that day. Now, on which day could he have said, "I told the truth yesterday."

What Day of the Week Is It? II

First, decide whether: (a) both statements are true; (b) both statements are false; or (c) one statement is true and one is false. Now ascertain the one day of the week that satisfies your conclusion.

What Day of the Week Is It? III

First, decide on what day or days A could have made his statement if (a) he were a Monday-Wednesday-Friday liar and (b) he were a Tuesday-Thursday-Saturday liar. Then do the same for B. Figure out on what day both statements could have been made.

What Day of the Week Is It? Is It Fair or Raining?

Prove that either A's statement is true and B's and C's are both false, or A's statement is false and B's and C's are both true. Once you have done this—and figured out which of the two alternatives is the case—you are well on your way to a solution.

Who Pilfered the Pies?

Assume Arn's statement is true. What conclusions does this lead to?

Who Stole the Bread?

Examine each statement and, using what you are told, determine which one of the three can be true.

The Missing Meat Pastries

Assume Arn's statement is true; what does that tell you about Con's statement?

The Doughnut Raid

List all the possible pairs of accomplices and use the given facts to eliminate those pairs that could not have made the theft.

A Master Robbery

First determine whether Arn is one of the two thieves.

A Princess or a Dragon? I

Sorry, no hint; any hint would be a giveaway of the answer.

A Princess or a Dragon? II

Focus, first, on the sign on the middle cave.

A Princess or a Dragon? III

Suppose both signs are false. Do you find a contradiction?

A Princess or a Dragon? IV

Suppose the sign on cave A is true. What conclusions do you reach?

Can a Fairy Say "I'm a Green Fairy?"

No hint; any hint would be a giveaway of the answer.

Pink or Green Fairy?

Assume that A is a real green fairy and look for contradictions.

Three Pink or Green Fairies

Consider whether it is possible for A and B to be different types of fairies.

Yellow or Blue? I

Review the logic of disjunction and conjunction (see page 38) if you are at all confused about this area of logic. Then, suppose the fairy's baton is a magic wand. Does that assumption lead to a conclusion about her type? Finally, suppose her baton is an ordinary stick. Does that assumption lead to a conclusion about her type?

Yellow or Blue? Magic Wand or Not? I

What happens if you assume the fairy's baton is magical?

Yellow or Blue? II

The amazing fact that is exemplified in this puzzle is that if Q is a statement, then any time a fairy says, "If I have a magic wand, then Q," Q must be true, whatever Q is. Can you prove this?

Yellow or Blue? Magic Wand or Not? II

Show that B must be carrying an ordinary stick. Use this fact to prove what kind of fairy B is. We are told that A is the other kind. Then evaluate A's statement knowing what kind she is.

Boots for the Ogres

What if the first three boots the ogre removes were three different colors?

Monster Heads/Monster Feet

I'm afraid this requires algebra, or a lot of trial-and-error.

King Arthur Meets with King Balfour

Choose the knight for seat #2 first. In how many ways may he be chosen? Now choose the knight for seat #3. He can be chosen in exactly the same number of ways as the knight for seat #2. Once you get to seat #3 you have a more limited number of ways of selecting the knight. How many are left to choose from? Continue from here.

Tending Horses

This puzzle requires some basic algebra. You will have four equations with four "unknowns." (See how helpful algebra can be?)

How Long Did Dob Walk?

Hint: Since Alicia and Dob arrived home ten minutes earlier than usual, Alicia drove for ten minutes less than usual. If you cannot come up with a general solution, try doing it by example. For example, you might suppose that Alicia's round trip (cottage to dock) is 60 minutes.

Magical Substance

When will the bowl be half full? Work backwards from this point.

Crossing the River

One of the knights must make the first trip. Who can be left alone with whom or what on this first trip?

The Farmer and the Hobgoblin

Figure out how many coins the farmer had just before the final doubling.

Wizard Rankings

From statement (1), there are two possibilities regarding the ranking changes of Fortuna and Deviner. One of these leads to a contradiction of another clue.

Minotaur Fighters

Start at the end and work toward the first lending.

To the King's Castle

Draw a diagram.

Building a Bridge

First figure out what part of the job Dobbit and Mobbit do in one hour when they work together.

What Time Does the Wagon Driver Leave His Hut?

First, figure out what part of the total trip the driver makes in the 10 minutes from 4:05 to 4:15.

Meeting the Stone Cutter

The cart driver spent 20 minutes less time traveling than he usually did. Of this 20 minutes, half would have been spent going toward the ferry and half coming from the ferry.

The Daughters of Alexis

Ten different combinations of three numbers add to 11, so the first clue is insufficient. You need to figure out why the next clue still fails to give sufficient information to Blythe.

How Far from Castleton to Devil's Peak?

Draw a diagram showing each rider's route.

Which Coin Is Lighter?

Divide the fifty coins into three groups: two with seventeen coins each and one with sixteen coins. The first weighing should compare the two groups of seventeen coins each.

In the Dark

Three. If the ogre pulled out only two boots, he might have had to wear one six-league and one seven-league boot. He took out three because at least two of the three would have to be the same type. The formula: N + 1 (N represents the number of types). 2 + 1 = 3.

Hidden Gold

The merchant divided the jars into groups of three and then set three jars aside. He placed three of the other six on each pan of the scale. They balanced, and so he knew that the jar with the gold was among the three jars he had not weighed. He put aside the six jars he had already weighed.

Next he took two of the three jars not yet weighed and placed them on each pan of the scale. He knew that if they balanced, the third jar was the one that held the gold.

But they did not balance. Then which was the jar with the gold? Was it the one that was heavier or lighter?

He removed the lighter jar and put it aside. Then he replaced it on the scale with one of the six jars he had weighed initially and which he knew did not contain the gold. When the two jars still did not balance, he knew the heavier jar held the gold.

A Master Robbery

The thieves were Birn and Dob. If Arn were one of the thieves, his statement would be false, so Con would be unable to ride and would be innocent. That would mean Con's statement was true; hence, Dob would be guilty. That means Dob's statement would have to be false. But Dob said that either Con was guilty or Arn was guilty, and, since Arn is guilty under our assumption, Dob's statement would be true. From this contradiction, we know that Arn must be innocent. If Birn is also innocent, then both Con and Dob are guilty. But that cannot be true since Con's statement would be true if Dob is innocent (i.e., this is a contradiction since the two thieves lied). So Birn must be guilty; hence Birn's statement is false. That means Con is innocent and Dob is guilty. (Note: this checks out, since both Dob's statement would be untrue and Con's statement would be true.)

Seven-League Boots

Six. Since he had only four six-league boots, if he took out six boots, he'd have at least one pair of seven-league boots.

In the Forest

Prince Benjamin. We know that Sir Kay shot down more than Princess Paula (statement 1), and that Prince Benjamin captured more than Sir Kay (statement 2). Therefore, Prince Benjamin captured more than either Sir Kay or Princess Paula.

In addition, we know that Princess Paula hit more than Prince Abel (statement 3). Therefore, Prince Benjamin was more successful than Sir Kay, Paula or Abel.

Sword Play

Four. The formula again: N + 1 (with N representing the types of ogre-fighters). If the swordsmith had pulled out two or three, he might have picked one of each type. Since he had only three types of weapons, with four he would have at least two of one type. He had three types of weapons and so N = 3. 3 + 1 = 4.

Captured!

Prince Abel's.

1.

Ben	Abel

Abel	Ben

2.

Abel	Ben	Paula

Paula	Ben	Abel

3.

Paula	Ben	Abel	Kay

Kay	Abel	Ben	Paula

Hidden Gold

The merchant divided the jars into groups of three and then set three jars aside. He placed three of the other six on each pan of the scale. The balanced, and so he knew that the jar with the gold was among the three jars he had not weighed. He put aside the six jars he had already weighed.

Next he took two of the three jars not yet weighed and placed them on each pan of the scale. He knew that if they balanced, the third jar was the one that held the gold.

But they did not balance. Then which was the jar with the gold? Was it the one that was heavier or lighter?

He removed the lighter jar and put it aside. Then he replaced it on the scale with one of the six jars he had weighed initially and which he knew did not contain the gold. When the two jars still did not balance, he knew the heavier jar held the gold.

The King's Heir

Both lied.

If you read the puzzle carefully, you'll see that the answer is obvious and that the puzzle doesn't require the involved solution that follows. It is included here only as an easy introduction to the method that is useful for more difficult puzzles.

	1	2	3	4
Black Hair	T	T	F	F
Red Hair	T	F	T	F

1. The first possibility indicates both princes were telling the truth. But we were told that at least one of them was lying.
2. We can eliminate both 2 and 3 because if either lied, the other could not have spoken the truth.
   If the prince with black hair lied when he said he was Abel, then he was Benjamin and the other prince must have been Abel.
   If the prince with red hair lied when he said he was Benjamin, then he must have been Abel and the other prince must have been Benjamin.
3. Therefore, both lied.

Baskets and Baskets

He balanced four of the baskets on each side of the scale. When they did not balance, he knew that the basket of pig food was among those on the heavier side of the scale.

If they had balanced, he would have known that the pig food was in the four that he did not weigh.

In either case, it took only one weighing for him to avoid the basket of pig fodder.

Which One Is the Knight?

C is a knight, A is a normal, B is a spy. One of the three is a knight, so C must be telling the truth. If not, then all three individuals are lying, and none could be a knight. Suppose B's statement is true. Then A is a knight. Since knights are always truthful, A's statement would be true: B would be a spy. But that presents us with the contradiction that a spy has made a true statement. So B's statement is untrue. Since C's statement is true, it follows that A's is also. Thus, B is a spy (since A's statement is true) and A is not a knight (since B's statement is false). So A must be a normal. C is, then, the knight.

The First Magic Number

75.

50	51	52	53	54	55	56	57	58	59
60	61	62	63	64	65	66	67	68	69
70	71	72	73	74	75	76	77	78	79

1. Condition A eliminates all multiples of 2 except those from 50 to 59. Eliminated therefore are 60, 62, 64, 66, 68 and 70, 72, 74, 76 and 78.

50	51	52	53	54	55	56	57	58	59
6̶0̶	61	6̶2̶	63	6̶4̶	65	6̶6̶	67	6̶8̶	69
7̶0̶	71	7̶2̶	73	7̶4̶	75	7̶6̶	77	7̶8̶	79

2. Condition B indicates that if the number was not a multiple of 3, it was a number from 60 through 69. This eliminates 50, 52, 53, 55, 56, 58, 59 and 71, 73, 77 and 79.

5̶0̶	51	5̶2̶	5̶3̶	54	5̶5̶	5̶6̶	57	5̶8̶	5̶9̶
6̶0̶	61	6̶2̶	63	6̶4̶	65	6̶6̶	67	6̶8̶	69
7̶0̶	7̶1̶	7̶2̶	7̶3̶	7̶4̶	75	7̶6̶	7̶7̶	7̶8̶	7̶9̶

3. Condition C indicates that if the number was not a multiple of 4, then it was a number from 70 through 79. This eliminates 51, 54, 57 and 61, 63, 65, 67 and 69.

5̶0̶	5̶1̶	5̶2̶	5̶3̶	5̶4̶	5̶5̶	5̶6̶	5̶7̶	5̶8̶	5̶9̶
6̶0̶	6̶1̶	6̶2̶	6̶3̶	6̶4̶	6̶5̶	6̶6̶	6̶7̶	6̶8̶	6̶9̶
7̶0̶	7̶1̶	7̶2̶	7̶3̶	7̶4̶	75	7̶6̶	7̶7̶	7̶8̶	7̶9̶

4. The remaining number, 75, satisfies all three conditions.
   A. It is not a multiple of 2 and so it does not have to be a number from 50 through 59.
   B. It is a multiple of 3, and so it does not have to be a number from 60 through 69.
   C. It is not a multiple of 4, and so it is, necessarily, a number from 70 through 79.

The Missing Swords

C. Number and direction are involved. There are three sets of single swords, three sets of double swords, but only two sets of three swords. None of the swords points downward.

The Ogre's Boast

100 or none.

	A	B	C	D	E	F	G	H
Ogre	T	T	T	T	F	F	F	F
Kay	T	T	F	F	T	T	F	F
Abel	T	F	F	T	T	F	T	F

1. We can eliminate A, B, D and E possibilities, because they indicate that two of the statements are true, and we are told that only one statement is true.
2. We can eliminate H, because it indicates that all the statements are false, and we know that one is true.
3. That leaves three possibilities: C, F and G.

	C	F	G
Ogre	T	F	F
Kay	F	T	F
Abel	F	F	T

4. If the ogre's claim that he devoured more than 100 is true, then Sir Kay's statement that the ogre ate *fewer* than 100 is false. But Abel's statement that the ogre ate at least one *can't* be false. So C is eliminated.
5. G need not be contradictory. Suppose the ogre's boast of more than 100 and Sir Kay's statement of less than 100 are false. Abel's statement that the ogre ate at least one could be true—if the ogre ate exactly 100.
6. As for F: if Sir Kay's statement that the ogre devoured fewer than 100 is true, then the ogre's claim is false. And Abel's statement that the ogre devoured at least one could also be false—if the ogre ate none!

Lead Weight

With the 1, 2, 4, and 8 ounce weights, the merchant could weigh any object from one ounce to 15 ounces.

Using weights of 1, 2 and the successive powers of 2, he could weigh up to, but not including, twice the heaviest weight. With two weights, 1 and 2, he could weigh up to and including 3 ounces.

With the 4-ounce weight, he could weigh, 4, 5 (4 + 1), 6 (4 + 2), and 7 (4 + 2 + 1).

With the 8-ounce weight, he could weigh 8, 9 (8 + 1), 10 (8 + 2), 11 (8 + 2 + 1), 12 (8 + 4), 13 (8 + 4 + 1), 14 (8 + 4 + 2), and 15 (8 + 4 + 2 + 1) ounces.

Wanted—Pig Food

It took two more weighings.

Dividing the heavier group of four baskets, he placed two on each side of the scale. The group of two that was heavier contained the pig fodder. He then put aside the two lighter baskets and divided the other two so that one was on each side of the scale. The one that was heavier this time was the pig fodder.

Heavier Stakes

1, 3, 9, and 27 pounds.

To weigh an object of two pounds, the merchant would add the 1-pound weight on the same side as the 2-pound object and balance it with the 3-pound weight on the other side: $2 = 3 - 1$.

To weigh a 4-pound object, he would balance the object with both the 1-pound and the 3-pound weight on the other side: $4 = 3 + 1$.

To weigh a 40-pound object, he would balance the object with all four weights on the other side: $4 = 1 + 3 + 9 + 27$.

Name the Knights

#1 is Black; #2 is Pure; #3 is Good; #4 is Glory; #5 is Bad; #6 is Grand; #7 is Noble; #8 is Brave; #9 is Chaste; #10 is White. From the preceding puzzle, we know that #1, #5, and #7 were the three knights who won one or more contests. From clues 1, 2, and 4, these three knights were, in some order, Sir Black, Sir Noble, and Sir Bad. The other seven knights were Sir Pure, Sir Brave, Sir Good, Sir Grand, Sir Chaste and Sir White, and Sir Glory. Sir Good's single contest was four matches before that between Sir Noble and Sir Bad (clue 3). Since both Sir Noble and Sir Bad won one or more contests, they have to have been #5 and #7 in one or the other order. Either way, Sir Good must have been #3, and Sir Black must have been #1 (previous puzzle's solution). Sir Noble defeated Sir Brave in Sir Brave's only contest (clue 2). Suppose Sir Noble had been #5 and Sir Bad #7. Then Sir Brave would have been #6. That would mean two knights whose names begin with "B" had consecutive numbers assigned to them (i.e., Sir Brave would have been #6, and Sir Bad would have been #7), contradicting clue 6. So Sir Noble was #7, Sir Bad was #5, and Sir Brave was not #6. Sir Brave was either #8 or #9 (clue 2). He can't have been #9, as then clue 5 couldn't be met. So Sir Brave was #8, whence, by clue 5, we know that Sir Chaste was #9 and Sir White was #10. Sir Bad defeated Sir Grand (clue 4), so, since Sir Grand won no contests, Sir Grand was #6. Sir Glory; then was #4 (clue 7). By elimination, Sir Pure was #2.

Weighty Matters

a) $9 - 3 - 1 = 5$ c) $27 = 27$
b) $27 - 9 - 3 - 1 = 14$ d) $27 - 3 + 1 = 25$

With the 9-pound weight, he could weigh objects from 5 pounds up to and including 13 pounds ($9 + 4$). To weigh a 5-pound object, he would place the 3-pound weight and the 1-pound weight on the same side as the object and balance it with the 9-pound weight ($9 - 3 - 1$). He used the same method for the 6-pound object ($9 - 3$).

To weigh a 7-pound object, he would place the 3-pound weight with the object and the 9-pound weight and the 1-pound weight on the other side ($9 + 1 - 3$). For an 8-pound object he would use ($9 - 1$); 10 ($9 + 1$); 11 ($9 + 3 - 1$); 12 ($9 + 3$); 13 ($9 + 3 + 1$).

And with the 27-pound weight he could weigh from 14 to 40 pounds ($13 + 27$). To weigh an object of 14 pounds, he would add to the object the 1, 3 and 9-pound weights while the 27-pound weight was on the other side: ($27 - 1 - 3 - 9$).

For a 15-pound object: ($27 - 3 - 9$); 16 ($27 - 3 - 9 + 1$); 17 ($27 - 1 - 9$); 18 ($27 - 9$); 19 ($27 - 9 + 1$); 20 ($27 - 9 - 1 + 3$); 21 ($27 - 9 + 3$); 22 ($27 - 9 + 3 + 1$); 23 ($27 - 1 - 3$); 24 ($27 - 3$); 25 ($27 - 3 + 1$); 26 ($27 - 1$); 27 (27); 28 ($27 + 1$); 29 ($27 - 1 + 3$); 30 ($27 + 3$); 31 ($27 + 3 + 1$); 32 ($27 + 9 - 3 - 1$); 33 ($27 + 9 - 3$); 34 ($27 + 9 + 1 - 3$); 35 ($27 + 9 - 1$); 36 ($27 + 9$); 37 ($27 + 9 + 1$); 38 ($27 + 9 + 3 - 1$); 39 ($27 + 9 + 3$); 40 ($27 + 9 + 3 + 1$).

Gold and Silver Coins

He took one coin from the first sack, two from the second, three from the third, and so on, until he had all ten from the tenth. Then he carefully stacked and weighed them.

In all he weighed 55 coins ($1 + 2 + 3 + 4 + 5 + 6 + 7 + 8 + 9 + 10$). Since each gold piece weighed ten grams, if all had been gold, the scale would have read 550 grams.

The amount by which the weight was too light indicated the number of silver coins and the number of the silver sack. For instance, if the weight was 543 grams, it would indicate that seven silver coins ($550 - 543 = 7$) had been weighed with the gold coins and that the rest of the silver coins were in the seventh sack.

The Second Magic Number

64. (See First Magic Number solution, page 96, for how-to-solve example.)

The Third Magic Number

44. (See First Magic Number solution, page 96, for how-to-solve example.)

Who Stole the Bread?

Con is the thief. If Arn were the thief, his statement would be true, contradicting the fact that the thief lied. So Arn's statement is false, and Arn is not the thief. This means that Birn told the truth when he said that Arn was lying. So Birn is not the thief. By elimination, Con is the thief (and he lied when he identified Birn as the thief).

The New Year's Eve Ball

First: Sir Good, white; second: Sir Venerable, blue; third: Sir Pure, gold; fourth: Sir Pious, purple. By clue 1, the four knights were Sir Pious, the knight who arrived second, the knight whose horse wore white trappings, and Sir Pure. These facts may be entered into a chart as shown:

	Knights	Order of Arrival	Color
1.	Pious		
2.		2nd	
3.			white
4.	Pure		

Since Sir Venerable's steed did not wear white trappings (clue 3), Sir Venerable must be the knight who arrived second. Thus, Sir Good rode the horse with white trappings. We now have:

	Knights	Order of Arrival	Color
1.	Pious		
2.	Venerable	2nd	
3.	Good		white
4.	Pure		

By clue 2, Sir Pious arrived fourth. Sir Good did not arrive third (clue 4), so he arrived first, and the horse with blue trappings was Sir Venerable's mount (also clue 4). Sir Pure arrived third (process of elimination). By clue 5, the horse with purple trappings wasn't ridden by Sir Pure, so it was Sir Pious's mount. Finally, the horse wearing gold trappings carried Sir Pure (process of elimination).

The Wizard Waves a Wand

C. Each dragon and knight moves to the left.

Merlin and the Disguises

Sir Good was disguised as Sir Kay, Sir Kay as Alt, Alt as Maj, Maj as Merlin, Merlin as Sir Good. We are told that each of the five was disguised as one of the other four, and that no two of the five were disguised as the same person. First, we determine which person was disguised as Merlin. That person was not Alt (clue 3). Suppose he had been Sir Good. Then, by clue 1, Merlin would have been disguised as Alt, so that, by clue 2, Alt would have been disguised as Sir Kay. But this would mean (clue 3) that Sir Kay as well as Sir Good portrayed Merlin. So we have a contradiction of what we are told. By similar reasoning, it was not Sir Kay who portrayed Merlin. For if it had been, then, by clue 3, Alt would have portrayed Sir Kay, so that, by clue 2, Merlin would have been disguised as Alt, whence, by clue 1, Sir Good as well as Sir Kay would have been disguised as Merlin. By elimination, it was the squire Maj who was disguised as Merlin. So Alt was disguised as Maj (clue 3). The person who was disguised as Alt was not Sir Good (clue 1). Suppose that person had been Merlin. Then Alt would have been disguised as Sir Kay as well as Maj (clue 2), a contradiction. So it was Sir Kay who was disguised as Alt. Thus, by clue 1, it was Sir Good who portrayed Sir Kay. By elimination (or by clue 2), Merlin was disguised as Sir Good.

Who Won the Jousting Tournament

Exactly three knights won one or more contests (clue 1). The first contest was between #1 and #2, so either #1 or #2 won at least one contest. A second winner was #5, since in order to have contested #6 (clue 2), #5 would have to have defeated a prior opponent. The third winner was #7, since #7 must have defeated #8 in order to have contested #9 (clue 3). By the rules and what we have deduced thus far, we know that #s 3 and 4 won no contests. Both were defeated by the same knight, either #1 or #2. By clue 4, that knight was #1. So #1 defeated #2, #3, and #4 in order. Then since clue 2 tells us that one contest was between #5 and #6, it follows that #1 lost when he fought #5. So the three winners of one or more matches were #1, #5, and #7. Thus, #5 must have defeated #6, only to have been overcome by #7, who must have gone on to defeat in turn, #s 8, 9, and 10, to win the tournament.

In summary, in the order of the matches:

> #1 defeated #2, #3, and #4 in succession
> #5 defeated #1 and #6 in succession
> #7 defeated, in order, #5, #8, #9, and #10

The Rankings of the Squires

The following chart summarizes the solution:

	Black	Good	Pure	Noble	Wise	Total
Gort	1	2	3	1	1	8
Harl	2	1	1	4	2	10
Jol	5	5	4	3	5	22
Kal	4	3	2	2	3	14
Lok	3	4	5	5	4	21

It is essential to use a chart, as suggested on page 84 of the Clues section. By clue 5, Sir Black and Sir Good gave scores of 5 to Jol. By clue 6, Sir Wise's 2 went to Harl, and Sir Noble's 2 went to Kal. Thus, Harl got a score higher than 2 from Sir Noble. By clue 4, that score was twice Sir Pure's score for Kal; so, Sir Noble gave Harl a 4, and Sir Pure gave Kal a 2. Lok received 21 points in total (clue 8). We now have:

	Black	Good	Pure	Noble	Wise	Total
Gort						
Harl				4	3	
Jol	5	5				
Kal			2	2		
Lok						21

To have achieved 21 points, Lok must have received one of the following sets of scores: (a) four 5's and one 1; (b) three 5's, one 4, and one 2; (c) three 5's and two 3's; (d) two 5's, two 4's, and one 3; (e) one 5 and four 4's. Since Jol got three scores of 5 (clue 5), we may eliminate (a), (b), and (c) by clue 8, Lok's score from Sir Black was lower than any other score he received, so we may eliminate (e). Thus, the true case is (d): Lok received two 5's, two 4's, and one 3. His 5's came from Sir Pure and Sir Noble (clue 7). By clue 8, he received a 3 from Sir Black. Thus, he received scores of 4 from Sir Good and Sir Wise. By clue 3, Kal received a 4 from Sir Black. So Sir Black gave his score of 2 to Harl (clue 1 and process of elimination), whence we may conclude that his score of 1 went to Gort, and Sir Good's score of 1 went to Harl. The chart should now read:

	Black	Good	Pure	Noble	Wise	Total
Gort	1					
Harl	2	1		4	2	
Jol	5	5				
Kal	4		2	2		
Lok	3	4	5	5	4	21

We now know that Gort is the squire whose highest score was a 3, given by Sir Pure (clue 9). Since Sir Wise gave Harl a 2 and Gort a score lower than 3, he can only have given Gort a score of 1. Jol's third score of 5 came from Sir Wise (process of elimination). So Sir Wise gave Kal a score of 3. Since Sir Noble gave Kal a 2 and Gort a score lower than 3, he gave Gort a 1; by elimination, he gave Jol a score of 3. The score Gort received from Sir Good is less than 3 and isn't 1, so it must have been 2. By elimination, Sir Good gave his score of 3 to Kal. By clue 2 and elimination, Sir Pure's score of 1 went to Harl, and his score of 4 went to Jol. The winner, then, was Jol with 22 points. Lok was second with 21 points, Kal third with 14, Harl fourth with 10, and Gort fifth with 8.

The Jousting Rankings

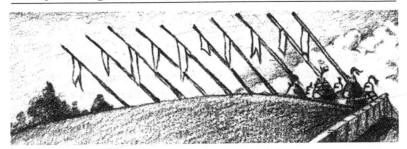

The year's rankings are:

1. Grand
2. Black
3. Balter
4. Pure
5. Glory
6. Good
7. Brave
8. White
9. Noble
10. Chaste

By clue 1, either (a) Pure went from #3 to #4 and Black from #6 to #2, or (b) Pure went from #3 to #8 and Black from #6 to #4. By clue 2, either (c) Chaste moved from #4 to #6 and Glory from #9 to #1, or (d) Chaste went from #4 to #8 and Glory from #9 to #3, or (e) Chaste went from #4 to #10 and Glory from #9 to #5. The possible combinations of (a) and (b) with (c), (d) and (e) are: (a) and (c); (a) and (d); (a) and (e); (b) and (c); (b) and (d); and (b) and (e).

The possibility of both (b) and (d) having occurred may be ruled out because that would put Pure and Chaste in the same position this year.

The possibility of both (a) and (d) having occurred, as well as that of (b) and (c) having occurred, are eliminated by clue 3a, since, by that clue, the two knights who switched positions were either #1, Good, and #2, Balter, or #7, White, and #8, Brave.

Let us suppose that (a) and (c) occurred: Pure moved from #3 to #4, Black from #6 to #2, Chaste from #4 to #6, and Glory from #9 to #1. Then the knights who switched positions (clue 3a) would have been White and Brave, while the knights of clues 3b and 3c would have been, respectively, Noble, moving from #10 to #9, and Balter, moving from #2 to #3. Then, Good, #1, would be the knight of clue 3e, moving from #1 to #5. By elimination of any other possibility, Grand would have moved from #5 to #10, but, by clue 4, this cannot have occurred.

Now suppose that both (b) and (e) occurred: Pure went from #3 to #8 and Black from #6 to #4, while Chaste went from #4 to #10 and Glory from #9 to #5. Then the two consecutively-ranked knights who switched positions would have been Good and Balter. To satisfy clue 3b, #7 would have moved to #6, or #8 would have moved to #7, or #10 would have moved to #9. If #7 had moved to #6, clue 3d could not be met. If #8 had moved to #7, then to satisfy clue 3c, #5 would have moved to #6. Then 3d cannot be met. If #10 had moved to #9, then to satisfy clue 3c, #5 would have moved to #6. Again, however, clue 3d cannot be met.

By elimination, the actual solution to clues 1 and 2 is (a) and (e): Pure moved from #3 to #4, Black from #6 to #2, Chaste from #4 to #10, and Glory from #9 to #5. Thus, by clue 3a, #7, Sir White and #8, Sir Brave, switched places in the rankings. Either Sir Good (#1) or Sir Grand (#5) moved to position 6 (clue 3d). In either case, the knight of clue 3c must be Sir Balter (#2 in the original rankings), who moved to position 3. Only Sir Noble can be the knight of clue 3b, moving from #10 to #9. Necessarily, then, since none of the knights retained his original ranking, #1, Good, moved to #6, and #5, Grand, to #1, and clues 3d and 3e are met.

What Day of the Week Is It? I

Sunday. If it were Tuesday, Thursday, or Saturday, days on which the inhabitant always tells the truth, he would not lie and say he had told the truth on the previous day. If it were Monday, Wednesday, or Friday, days on which he always lies, he would not say he had told the truth on the previous day—for such a statement would be true. It is Sunday, a day on which the inhabitant tells the truth, and the only day of the week on which it is true that he tells the truth on the preceding day.

Can a Fairy Say "I'm a Green Fairy?"

No. If the pink-looking fairy were a real pink fairy, she would tell the truth and would not say that she is a green fairy, and if she were really a green fairy, she would not truthfully say that she was.

Deeds of Derring-Do

First deed: Sir Gallant, killing giant, Frey, south; 2nd deed: Sir Chivalrous, killing Saxon spy, Golan, east; 3rd deed: Sir Bountiful, slaying dragon, Damon, north; 4th deed: Sir Daring, killing evil knight, Alain, west. By clue 4, the deed of Sir Chivalrous, who was served by Golan, was the second of the four to be accomplished. By clue 3, the deed of Sir Bountiful and that accomplished in a spot east of the future Camelot were consecutive deeds in one or the other order, and both were accomplished before Alain's knight went on his mission to kill the evil knight. So Sir Chivalrous, Alain's knight, and Sir Bountiful are three of the knights. Alain's knight's deed was either the third or last to be accomplished, and Sir Chivalrous's deed was the second of the four accomplished. So Sir Chivalrous's deed is one of the two mentioned in clue 3, and can only be the one undertaken east of the future Camelot. By clue 2, Frey's knight, who wasn't Sir Bountiful, accomplished the first deed: killing the giant. So Bountiful's deed was the third of the four, and Alain's knight's deed the last of the four. Sir Bountiful's squire can only have been Damon (process of elimination). By clue 5, Sir Bountiful's deed took place north of the future Camelot. By clue 6, Sir Gallant was served by Frey, and Alain's knight, who, by elimination, was Sir Daring, accomplished his heroic act west of the future Camelot. Sir Galant's deed was undertaken south of the future Camelot (process of elimination).

Finally, by clue 1, only Bountiful could have slain the dragon. By elimination, Sir Chivalrous defeated the Saxon spy.

A Princess or a Dragon? IV

Caves B and C contain the princesses. Suppose the sign on cave A is true, so that cave B contains a dragon. Then the sign on cave B is false (because cave B contains a dragon), and so cave C contains a dragon (because the sign on B, which, under our assumption, is false, says that cave C does not contain a dragon). Then, since cave C contains a dragon, the sign on cave C must be false; but that is a contradiction, since, under our assumption that the statement on cave A is true, cave B contains a dragon.

So we have shown that the sign on cave A must be false. Therefore, cave B contains a princess, and therefore it bears a sign with a true statement. Since the statement on cave B is true, it follows that cave C contains a princess and bears a sign with a true statement (which checks out, since, from what we are told, the second dragon must be in cave D; note that the sign on cave D is false, which checks out, since cave C does not contain a dragon).

The Pavilions of the Champions

A: Sir Good, oak tree, Hab; B: Sir Chaste, lion, Bran; C: Sir Pure, bear, Col; D: Sir Brave, falcon, Altur; E: Sir White, dragon, Fel. By clue 3, pavilion C belonged to the knight whose emblem was the bear. By clue 4, Sir White's pavilion was E, Altur was the squire at pavilion D, and the oak tree was the emblem of the knight at pavilion A. Bran was the squire at B (clue 5). By clue 6, the knight at D had the emblem of the falcon. Sir Chaste had pavilion B (clue 9). Sir Brave's pavilion was not C (clue 1) or A (clue 2), so Sir Brave had pavilion D. Col's knight had pavilion C (clue 1). Fel's knight did not have pavilion A (clue 5), so Fel's knight had pavilion E, and Hab's knight, by elimination, had pavilion A. By clue 7, the lion was not Sir White's emblem, so the knight whose emblem is the lion had pavilion B, and the dragon, by elimination, was the emblem of pavilion E's knight. By clue 8, Sir Good's pavilion was A. By elimination, Sir Pure's was C.

Knights, Normals, and Spies I

A is the knight, B is the spy, C is the normal. We know that exactly one of the three is a knight and one a spy. The knight can't be C since, if C were a knight, his statement would be a true statement; therefore, B would also be a knight. Now, suppose B is the knight. Then C's statement would be true, so C would not be the spy, exactly what A said. So A's statement would be true also, so none of the three could be a spy, contrary to what we are told. So B is not the knight. So A must be the knight. Now B's statement is false, and as B is not a knight, C's statement is false. But, from A's statement, C is not a spy, so C is the normal, and B is the spy.

106

A Princess or a Dragon? I

Cave A does not contain a dragon; cave B does. One of the signs is false and the other true. Since one of the caves contains a dragon, the sign on cave A is necessarily true. Since only one of the signs is true, the one on cave B is false. The dragon, then, is in cave B.

Three Pink or Green Fairies

A and B are pink; C is green; A appears to be green. We show that A and B must be the same kind of fairy (in essence, that is, not necessarily in appearance). Suppose they are two different types. First, suppose A is pink and B is green. This cannot be the case, because if A were a pink fairy; she would not make the false statement that B is pink. Now, suppose A is green and B is pink. This cannot be the case either, because if A were a green fairy, she would not make the true statement that B is pink. So A and B are either both pink fairies or both green fairies. Suppose they are both green. Then A is green, so the "if" part of B's statement ("A is a pink fairy") is false. This means (recalling the discussion of logical implication) that B's statement is true, a contradiction of the assumption that B is a green fairy. So both A and B are pink fairies. Therefore since A is a pink fairy and B has made a true "if-then" statement, it follows that C is a green fairy.

Then, remembering what it means for an "or" statement to be false, we know that both parts of C's statement are false (since C is green). Hence, "A is what she appears to be" is a false statement. So A must appear to be green.

The Three Suspects

We show that if A had said that he was a knight, the judge would not have been able to positively identity a spy among the three prisoners. In this case, any one of the three could be a spy. The first prisoner could be a spy and either one of the others could be a knight. The second prisoner could be a spy if the first is a knight and the third a normal (lying on this occasion). The third prisoner could be a spy and either the first or second a knight. So A must have said "I'm a normal." Now if A's statement is true, he is a normal, so both B's and C's statements would be false, and we would be left with no knight among the three. So A's statement must be false; he is not a normal, but he lied, so he must be a spy. So B's and C's statements are both true. The judge could not have known which of B and C was a knight and which was a normal, but of course, the judge has done his duty by determining that A is the only spy.

What Day of the Week Is It? II

Friday. Clearly these statements were not made on Sunday, the one day of the week on which all inhabitants tell the truth. On any other day of the week, one of the inhabitants tells the truth and the other lies, so one statement must be true and the other false. Suppose A's statement is the true statement; then yesterday was Sunday, and today is Monday. But A lies on Mondays, so this cannot be the case. So A's statement is false. Thus, B's statement is true: tomorrow is Saturday and today is Friday. (B tells the truth on Fridays and A lies on Fridays, so there is no contradiction.)

A Lame Horse

10 times. The knight walked two-thirds of the distance and rode one-third of it, so he walked twice as far as he rode. The walking portion took twenty times as long as the riding portion; so, if the walking and riding distances had been the same, the walking part would have taken ten times as long as the riding part. Thus, the knight rode ten times as fast as he walked.

Who Pilfered the Pies?

Arn is definitely guilty. Assume Arn's statement is the one of the three that is true. Then Arn is not guilty, so both Birn and Con are guilty. But that means that both Birn's and Con's statements would be true. This is a contradiction of what we are told (i.e., that just one of the three statements is true). So Arn's statement is false. Therefore Arn is guilty. Attempts to discover whether Birn or Con is the other guilty one are unfruitful. If the one true statement were made by Birn, then Con is guilty, and if it were made by Con then Birn is guilty. Since we have no means of determining which of the two made the true statement, we cannot determine whether it is Birn or Con who is the other thief.

Knights, Normals, and Spies II

A is the normal, B is the spy, C is the knight. A knight would not say that he is a normal, so B cannot be the knight. Nor can B be the normal, for then, B's statement would be true, whence both A's and C's would also be true-contradiction since at least one of the statements is false (the one made by the spy). So B is the spy, and his statement is false. Thus, A's statement is false, so A is the normal of the three. Finally, C is the knight (the "his statement is false" part of C's statement is true, making the entire statement true).

Monster Heads/Monster Feet

30 of the monsters with two heads and three feet each, 20 of the others. This puzzle is most easily solved by using algebra. If x = the number of monsters with two heads and three feet each, and y = the number of monsters with three heads and four feet each, then, from the given facts we have:

(1) $2x + 3y = 120$
(2) $3x + 4y = 170$

Now multiply each member of the first equation by 3 and each member of the second by –2 and add together the resulting equivalent equations, as follows, to obtain y = 20:

(1a) $6x + 9y =$ 360
(2a) – $6x – 8y = –$ 340
                  $y =$ 20

Since y = 20, we have, from the original equation 1, $2x + 3(20) = 120$, $2x + 60 = 12$, $2x = 60$, $x = 30$.

Feeding the Horses

Yes. Sixty-nine days of winter remain, and enough food is on hand to feed the two remaining horses for 72 days. This puzzle can be solved using algebra, but I like the following solution: When the four horses were sold, Distal had been feeding his original six horses for 6 days. Had he kept all six horses, he would have been able to feed them for another 24 days. But as he had only two horses—one-third as many—the food will last three times as long, or 72 days.

Yellow or Blue, Magic Wand or Not?

Yellow fairy/ordinary stick. If she were carrying a magic wand her statement would be true, so both parts would be true (The "I am carrying an ordinary stick" part as well as the "I am a blue fairy" part). This can't be the case, so she must be carrying an ordinary stick. Thus, her (compound) statement is false, which means one or the other part of it is false, or both parts are false. We know that the "I am carrying an ordinary stick" part is true, so it must be false that she is a blue fairy; so she is a yellow fairy.

The Genie and the Coins

A. Double the number of coins in the preceding box and add 1 (2 + 1 = 3, 6+ 1 = 7, 14 + 1 = 15, 30 + 1 = 31).

Chased by a Glub

Since Phipos first ran half the time it took him to reach the fort, he ran for more than half the distance. So, when half the distance had been covered, Phipos was still running, but the glub had begun to walk. Therefore, the glub fell farther and farther behind Phipos. When Phipos began to walk, the glub was still walking, so the distance Phipos gained while he ran and the glub walked was maintained.

What Day of the Week Is It? III

Monday. From puzzle 5, we know that if A were a Monday–Wednesday –Friday liar, he could make the statement, "I told the truth yesterday," only on a Sunday. However, if A were a Tuesday–Thursday–Saturday liar, he could have made his statement only on Monday. So either:

A is a Mon.–Wed.–Fri. liar and spoke on Sunday, <u>or</u>
A is a Tues.–Thurs.–Sat. liar and spoke on Monday.

If B were a Mon.–Wed.–Fri. liar, he could have said, "Yesterday was Monday," on a Monday, a Wednesday, or Friday because the statement would have been a lie on those days. Or, he could have said it on a Tuesday, because the statement would be true on a day when he tells the truth. On the other hand, if B were a Tues.–Thurs.–Sat. liar, he could have made the statement "Yesterday was Monday," only on a Thursday or Saturday, the only days on which it is a fact both that he lies and the statement is a lie. He couldn't have made it on a Monday, Wednesday, or Friday because the statement would be false on a day when he tells the truth. So, either:

B is a Mon.–Wed.–Fri. liar and spoke on Monday, Tuesday, Wednesday, or Friday, <u>or</u> B is a Tues.–Thurs.–Sat. liar and spoke on Thursday, or Saturday.

We seek a day of the week on which both statements could be made, one by one type and the second by the other type of liar. Obviously the only day that could be, would be Monday, and only if A is a Tues.–Thurs.–Sat. liar and B a Mon.–Wed.–Fri. liar.

The Missing Meat Pastries

Arn is guilty. If Arn's statement is the one that is true, then Arn is innocent (since only one of the three is the thief), so Con's statement is true also. We cannot have two statements true, so Arn's statement is false. Since the content of Arn's statement is false, neither Birn nor Con is guilty and Arn is. The one who made a true statement is Birn.

Yellow or Blue? I

Blue fairy (it cannot be determined whether she carries a magic wand or an ordinary stick). Suppose the fairy's baton is a magic wand. Then, because she carries a magic wand we know her statement is true, meaning that at least one part is true:

"I am a blue fairy and I have a magic wand" is true, <u>or</u>
"I am a yellow fairy and I have an ordinary stick" is true.

The second part is false because we have assumed she is carrying a magic wand. So the first part is true; she is a blue fairy.

Now suppose the fairy is carrying an ordinary stick. Then, because she is carrying an ordinary stick, her statement is false. This means both parts of her statement are false: she is not a blue fairy with a magic wand, and she is not a yellow fairy with an ordinary stick. Since she does have an ordinary stick, it is obvious she is not a blue fairy with a magic wand. But since she also is not a "yellow fairy with an ordinary stick," she must be a blue fairy with an ordinary stick, as that is the only way the statement, "I am a yellow fairy and I am carrying an ordinary stick" can be false.

The Doughnut Raid

The thieves are Birn and Dob. The two were not Arn and Con, or Arn and Dob (statement 1), or Birn and Cob (statement 2), or Arn and Birn (statement 3), or Con and Dob (statement 4). By elimination, they were Birn and Dob.

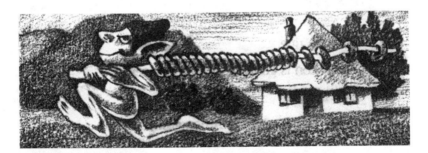

Weighing a Pound of Flour

She put the one-pound weight on one pan of the scale and balanced it with lead pellets placed on the other pan. She then removed the one-pound weight and replaced it with flour until it balanced the lead pellets.

A Princess or a Dragon? III

Both caves contains princesses. Suppose both signs bore false statements. Then, by the false statement on cave B, cave A contains a dragon. But that means that the statement on cave A is true, a contradiction. So both signs have true statements on them. By the true statement on cave B, cave A contains a princess. By the true sign on cave A, cave B contains a princess.

Boots for the Ogres

Eight. If the first three boots removed from the chest happened to be three different colors, then a fourth boot must be removed to obtain the first pair of boots of the same color. Assume this is the case, and assume, without loss of generality, that the fourth boot is black. The boots removed at this point would be: one white boot, one brown boot, one pair (two) black boots. Then, suppose that the fifth boot is black, which could be the case, since there are three boots of each color in the chest. Thus, the first five boots removed from the chest would consist of: one white boot, one brown boot, three black boots. So a sixth boot would have to be removed in order to guarantee a second pair. Since the three black boots have all been removed, the sixth boot would have to be either white or brown. Without loss of generality, assume it is brown. So the boots removed to this point would consist of: 3 black boots, 2 brown boots, one white boot. Then, if the seventh boot happened to be brown, the boots removed at this point would be: 3 black boots, 3 brown boots, one white boot. Thus, an eighth boot would have to be removed in order to obtain a third pair of matching boots—which, of course, under our without-loss-of-generality assumptions, would be white.

Pink or Green Fairy?

A is as she appears to be, a pink fairy; B is really a green fairy. Suppose A is a green fairy. Then A's statement is a lie, so B is a pink fairy. This leads us to the contradiction that B is a pink fairy who has made a false statement. So A must be a pink fairy. Therefore, A's statement that B is a green fairy is true (which checks out without contradiction, since B's statement is false).

How Long Did Dob Walk?

55 minutes. Since Alicia and Dob arrived home ten minutes earlier than usual, Alicia drove ten minutes less than usual. So she drove one way—towards the ferry dock—for five minutes less than usual. Had she driven for the other five minutes, she would have arrived at the ferry dock at the usual time, one hour later than Dob's actual time of arrival on this particular day. So Dob must have walked for 55 minutes. If you don't understand this, don't be dismayed. It is not an easy problem.

Let's look at an example, just to convince you that 55 minutes is the correct answer. Suppose that the time required for one round trip for Alicia is 60 minutes (30 minutes each way). Also, without loss of generality, suppose that she usually leaves the cottage at 6:00, thus arriving at the ferry dock at 6:30 and arriving back home with Dob at 7:00. On the day in question, she leaves at her usual time, 6:00 but she and Dob arrive home at 6:50. Dob arrived at the ferry dock at 5:30 and began walking. Alicia's total round-trip time is 50 minutes, so she drove the mule for 25 minutes before she met Dob. She left home at 6:00 and met Dob at 6:25. Dob had been walking since 5:30, a total of 55 minutes. Try this with a different set of assumptions and you will still arrive at 55 minutes for an answer.

How Many Cakes?

24 cakes; each being took 6. Heartnik took 1/4 the original number, leaving 3/4 of that number. Scowler took 1/3 of that 3/4, or 1/4 of the original number. So, after Heartnik and Scowler had helped themselves, 1/2 the original number of cakes remained on the plate. Goodin took 1/2 of that half, so he, as well as Heartnik and Scowler, took 1/4 of the original number. Thus, after Goodin had helped himself, 1/4 the original number remained. So Loglob, the last being to take the cakes, took 1/4 the original number. As he took six cakes, there were 24 cakes in the beginning, and each being took six.

Crossing the River

Sir Good rows the corn over, leaves it, and rows back alone. Then Sir Pure rows the ogre over, leaves the ogre with the corn, and rows back alone. Sir Good and Sir Pure then row over together (leaving the goose behind). Sir Pure stays with the corn and the ogre. Sir Good rows back, picks up the goose, and rows across the river.

Genie Horseplay

B. The horse immediately to the left of the genie grows. The horse to the immediate right of the genie shrinks.

Yellow or Blue? II

Yellow. Suppose that the fairy carries a magic wand. Then the statement, "If I have a magic wand, I am a yellow fairy," must be true (since fairies with magic wands always tell the truth). So the "then" part of her statement would be true: she would be a yellow fairy. Therefore, it is proved that if she carries a magic wand she is a yellow fairy. But that is precisely what she asserted. Therefore, she made a true statement, so she must carry a magic wand. And since we have proved that if she carries a magic wand she is yellow, then it must be true that she is yellow.

Building a Bridge

15 hours. For each hour that Dobbit worked, 1/30 of the project was completed. So after Dobbit had worked 5 hours alone, 5(1/30), or 1/6, of the job was completed, leaving 5/6 of the job for Dobbit and Mobbit to do together. For each hour that Mobbit worked, he did 1/45 of the job. For each hour the two worked together, the part of the job that was done was 1/30 + 1/45 = 5/90, which reduces to 1/18. So, together, the two would do the entire job in 18 hours. Thus, to do 5/6 of it required 5/6 × 18 = 15 hours.

How Can Everyone Cross the River?

The half-elf rows the human across to Tok, leaving the dwarf and the elf at Ak. The half-elk leaves the human at Tok and returns to Ak alone. On his next trip the half-elf rows the dwarf across, leaving the elf alone at Ak. The half-elf leaves the dwarf in Tok and returns to Ak with the human. Leaving the human at Ak, the half-elf rows the elf across the river and leaves the elf with the dwarf at Tok. On the last trip the half-elf takes the human across again to Tok.

Tending Horses

The puzzle can best be solved by using algebra. If we let a = the number of mares Aken tends, b = the number of mares Col tends, c = the number of stallions Aken tends, and d = the number of stallions Col tends, we obtain four equations in four unknowns:

(1) $b = 2a$
(2) $c = 4a$
(3) $c = d + 2$
(4) $d = b + 2$

Using the fact that b = 2a (equation 1), by substitution of 2a for b in equation 4, we obtain:

(5) $d = 2a + 2$

From equation 2, c = 4a, so substituting 4 a for c in equation 3, we obtain:

(6) $4a = d + 2$

Equation 6 may also be written:

(7) $d = 4a - 2$

Then, by substitution, using equations 5 and 7, we obtain: $2a + 2 = 4a - 2$. Then, by arithmetic, $2a = 4$, so $a = 2$. The rest is obtained by substitution. Since a = 2, b = 4 (equation 1). Since a = 2, c = 8 (equation 2). Since b = 4, d = 6 (equation 4).

The Farmer and the Hobgoblin

15 coins. To solve the puzzle start at the end. Since the farmer gave the hobgoblin his "last sixteen coins," sixteen is the number of coins the farmer had after the final doubling; so, he had eight coins when he crossed the field for the last time. Add to this the sixteen he gave the hobgoblin after the third crossing, and the result is twenty-four, which is twice the number of coins he had before the third crossing.

So the farmer had twelve coins when he started the third crossing. Adding to twelve coins the sixteen he gave the hobgoblin after the second crossing gives twenty-eight coins, which is twice the number he had before the second crossing.

So he started the second crossing with fourteen coins. Add to fourteen the sixteen coins he gave the hobgoblin after the first crossing, and the result is thirty, which is twice the number of coins he started with. Thus, the farmer began the first crossing with fifteen coins.

Yellow or Blue, Magic Wand or Not? II

A is a yellow fairy carrying an ordinary stick; B is a blue fairy carrying an ordinary stick. B cannot be carrying a magic wand, for if so she would be a "truther," hence wouldn't say she is carrying an ordinary stick. So B is carrying an ordinary stick, which means B always lies. Since it's true that she carries an ordinary stick, the only way she can be lying is if she is a blue fairy. Now consider A. Since the two fairies are of different colors, A is a yellow fairy. Since A is a yellow fairy, her statement that she is a blue fairy carrying a magic wand is false. Then, since she made a false statement, she must be carrying an ordinary stick (since fairies with magic wands do not make false statements). Looking at the analysis with respect to A in another way: knowing that A is a yellow fairy, could a yellow fairy with a magic wand have made the statement A made? Clearly the answer is "No." Hence A has an ordinary stick.

What Day of the Week Is It? Is It Fair or Raining?

It is a clear Saturday. It cannot be a Sunday, clear or rainy, since A tells the truth on Sunday, whereas, "It is raining and today is Tuesday" is only true on a rainy Tuesday. So, since the three statements were made on a day other than Sunday, either A's statement is true (it's a rainy Tuesday) and both B's and C's are false, or A's statement is false and both B's and C's are true. Now A's statement cannot be true, for then B's would also be true (because the "It is Tuesday" portion of it would be true. Therefore, A's statement is false, and both B's and C's are true. Any false statement made by A was made on a fair Tuesday, Thursday, or Saturday, or on a rainy Monday, Wednesday, or Friday. Any true statement made by B was made on a fair Tuesday, Thursday, or Saturday, or on a rainy Monday, Wednesday, or Friday. But, since B's statement is known to be true as to its content, it could not have been made on a rainy Monday, Wednesday, or Friday. So B's statement was made, and A's statement was made, on a fair Tuesday, Thursday, or Saturday. The only one of those days on which C's statement is true, as it must be, is a clear Saturday (on a clear Tuesday, his statement would be false because tomorrow would be Wednesday, while on a clear Thursday, his statement would be false because tomorrow would be Wednesday, while on a clear Thursday, his statement would be false because the previous day was Wednesday).

How Much Did Alaranthus Weigh?

3000 pounds. Alaranthus's weight was such that 1000 pounds was equal to one-third of his weight. So his total weight in pounds was 3×1000.

Wizard Rankings

The latest rankings are: 1. Chameleoner, 2. Alchemerion, 3. Elvira, 4. Fortuna, 5. Bogara, 6. Deviner.

From statement (2) either Fortuna's ranking changed from 6 to 2 and Deviner's from 4 to 3, or Fortuna changed from 6 to 4 and Deviner from 4 to 6. If the former were the actual case, then Fortuna's change would have been a four-step change. But Bogara's ranking could not have changed by more than four steps, so a four-step change in Fortuna's ranking would lead to a contradiction of statement (1). So Fortuna's ranking changed from 6 to 4 and Deviner's from 4 to 6.

From statement (1), Bogara's ranking changed from 2 to 5, a three-step change. Since Elvira's change in ranking was smaller than Bogara's, her ranking changed to 3. All the rankings changed, so Alchemerion's new ranking was 2 and Chameleoner, by elimination, went to the top spot, ranking 1.

How Far Apart Were the Dragons?

5 miles. To solve this puzzle, the formula d = rt (distance = rate multiplied by time) is used. The dragons' rates are stated as miles per hour, so time must be expressed in terms of hours in order to obtain a meaningful answer. Five minutes = 1/12 hour, so the distance Argothel walked in 5 minutes at a rate of 24 miles per hour was 2 miles (24 × 1/12), while the distance Bargothel walked was 3 miles (36 × 1/12). So the dragons were 5 miles apart 5 minutes before they met.

A Round-Table Arrangement

1, Hob; 2, Rob; 3, Cob; 4, Bob; 5, Tob; 6, Lob.

Cob doesn't have seat #1 (clue 3). From clue 2, either Hob or Lob has that seat. Suppose it is Lob who has the #1 seat. Then Hob would have the #6 seat and Cob the #4 seat (clue 2). Rob would then have seat #3 (clue 3), and Bob would have the #5 seat (clue 1). By elimination, Tob would have seat #2, contradicting clue 4.

So Hob must have seat #1. Cob and Lob have seats #3 and #6 in one order or the other (clue 2). Suppose Lob has seat #3 and Cob seat #6. Then, by clue 1, Bob would have seat #5, while by clue 3, Rob would have seat #5. Thus, Cob has seat #3 and Lob seat #6. By clue 3, Rob has seat #2. Bob has seat #4 (clue 1). By elimination, Tob has seat #5.

```
          M
          1
   7            2

6               3

    5       4
```

What Time Does the Wagon Driver Leave His Hut?

The driver leaves his hut at 3:50 P.M. and arrives at the dock at 5:05 P.M. In the 10 minutes from 4:05 to 4:15, he goes $1/3 - 1/5 = 2/15$ the distance. So in 5 minutes, he goes 1/15 the distance, and in 15 ($15 \times 5 = 75$) minutes he goes the full distance. At 4:15 he has made 1/3 of the trip, which has taken $1/3(75) = 25$ minutes. So he leaves his hut at 3:50 and arrives at the dock 75 minutes later, at 5:05.

Magical Substance

1/8 full. At the end of the third day the bowl is half full (since it doubles its volume each day). So at the end of the second day it is 1/4 full (since $2 \times 1/4 = 1/2$ at the end of the third day). Thus, at the end of the first day it is 1/8 full (since $2 \times 1/8 = 1/4$ at the end of the second day).

How Far from Castleton to Devil's Peak?

Castleton and Devil's Peak are 10 miles apart. The rider who started his journey at Devil's Peak rode 1 1/2 times as fast as the rider who started his trip at Castleton.

The diagram below shows that when the horsemen met for the first time, they had, together, traveled a distance equal to the distance between Castleton and Devil's Peak. When they met for the second time, they had traveled, together, three times the distance between the two towns.

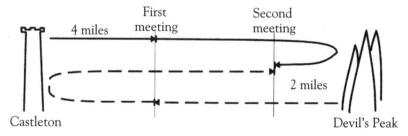

Both riders traveled at a constant speed, so when they met the second time, each had ridden three times as far as he had when the two met the first time. The rider who began at Castleton had, thus, traveled $3 \times 4 = 12$ miles. The distance of 12 miles is 2 miles more than the distance between the towns, so the towns are 10 miles apart.

As for the two riders' relative speed, during the time that the rider who began the trip at Castleton rode 4 miles, the other rider rode 6 miles. So the other rider rode 1 1/2 times as fast.

Meeting the Stone Cutter

5.50 A.M. the cart would normally have arrived at the ferry landing at 6:00 A.M. But on the day in question, the cart driver delivered the stone worker to the quarry 20 minutes early, so the driver spent 20 minutes less time traveling than he usually did: 10 minutes going toward the ferry and 10 minutes going to the quarry. Subtract 10 minutes from 6:00 A.M. to get 5:50 A.M., as the time the cart met the worker.

If you find this difficult to follow, let's say that normally the driver leaves the quarry at 5:00 A.M. in order to arrive at the ferry at 6:00 A.M. and deliver the worker to the quarry at 7:00 A.M. In other words the cart driver drives one hour each way on a normal day. But on the day in question, the cart driver delivered the worker to the quarry at 6:40. The cart driver left for the ferry at his usual time, 5:00 A.M., and drove until 6:40, so he drove for 100 minutes, 50 minutes in one direction and 50 in another. Normally he drives 60 minutes to reach the ferry landing. Thus, he drove for 10 fewer minutes toward the ferry landing. So he must have picked up the worker at 5:50 A.M. rather than 6:00 A.M.

How Did the Archers Cross the River?

First, the two children rowed the boat across. One child remained on the river's far side while the second child rowed back to the archers. An archer then rowed across alone. This archer sent the boat back with the child who had remained on the far side of the river. The two children then rowed across again, and again one remained on the far side while the other rowed back. Next, a second archer rowed across, and sent the boat back with the child who had been left on the far side of the river. This process was repeated until all the archers were across.

How Early Was the Barge?

20 minutes early. The cart driver traveled 24 minutes less than usual. If he had not met the rider, he would have needed half of those minutes, 12 minutes, to get to the dock at his usual time. But the rider had ridden for 8 minutes before he and the cart driver met, so the barge was 12 + 8 = 20 minutes early.

The Sons of Blythe

They are 2, 3, and 6 years old. Since all three are younger than 10 years of age, and the product of the ages of the two youngest equals the age of the oldest, the ages are 2, 2, 4; or 2, 3, 6; or 2, 4, 8; or 3, 3, 9. Of these, only 2, 3, and 6 add up to a number that is a prime number.

Human Population of South Pymm

389. The population of North Pymm is smaller than 500 and is a number that has 3, 4, 5 and 7 as integral factors (i.e., 3, 4, 5, and 7 divide into the number without a remainder). Since 3, 4, 5, and 7 are relatively prime, the smallest possible number is the product of 3, 4, 5, and 7, which is 420. The next largest possible number would be 840, which is too large. So the population of North Pymm is 420 and the population of South Pymm is $(1/3)\ 420 + (1/4)\ 420 + (1/3)\ 420 + (1/7)\ 420 = 140 + 105 + 84 + 60 = 389$.

Measuring Two Gallons of Cider

Fill the 3-gallon container with cider and empty it into the 4-gallon container. Fill the 3-gallon container a second time and pour it into the 4-gallon container. When the 4-gallon container is full, 2 gallons remain in the 3-gallon container.

Rings for the Princesses

King Firnal can bestow two princesses with rings and then give the box with the remaining ring to the third princess.

The Daughters of Alexis

The girls are 1, 2, and 8 years old. Blythe could not answer the question using the first clue because ten different combinations of three numbers add to 11 (1, 1, 9; 1, 2, 8; 1, 3, 7; 1, 4, 6; 1, 5, 5; 2, 2, 7; 2, 3, 6; 2, 4, 5; 3, 3, 5; 3, 4, 4).

Since the second clue did not provide Blythe with the answer, it must be the case that at least two combinations from the list above have a product which is either 16 years more or 16 years less than Blythe's age. The products derived from the list above are, in the order of the list, 9, 16, 21, 24, 25, 28, 36, 40, 45, 48. Since no two of these products are the same, it must be true that one product is 16 more and the other is 16 less than Blythe's age. Thus, the difference between these two products is 32.

Comparing each product with each of the others, we find two products that meet this requirement: 16 and 48, the products of 1, 2, and 8, and 3, 4, and 4, respectively (thus, Blythe is 32 years old). Blythe could not determine the children's age even with this second clue. However, Alexis's third statement revealed that there was a daughter whose age was greater than the others, so the 3, 4, 4 combination was ruled out.

Inspecting the Troops

59 seconds. The answer is not 58 seconds (twice 29 seconds). Refer to the distance between the first and second troop, or second and third troop, etc., one segment. There are twenty-nine segments between the first and thirtieth man. The time required was 29 seconds to cover this distance, so the officer rides at the rate of 1 second per segment. There are fifty-nine segments in total, so the total time required will be 59 seconds.

How Many Schlockels?

Altus has 32 schlockels. From clue 1, if the number of schlockels Altus has is a multiple of 5, the number is 5, 10, 15. However, from clue 2, the number is not 5, 10, or 15, because none of these is a multiple of 8 and none is between 20 and 29. So the number of schlockels Altus has is not a multiple of 5. From this we know that it is also not a multiple of 10—since any number that is a multiple of 10 is a multiple of 5. Hence, from clue 3, Altus has 31, 32, 33, 34, 36, 37, 38, or 39 schlockels. The number cannot be "not a multiple of 8," so it is a multiple of 8. Thus, Altus has 32 schlockels.

Human vs. Minotaur

The human warrior's clockwise counting should begin with the warrior third from the Minotaur moving clockwise. He numbers the positions 1 to 7 as in the arrangement below, with M, the Minotaur's position, labeled "1." He would then start counting seven places beginning with "4." This lands him on "3." He defeats "3," then, beginning with "4," he counts clockwise another seven places. This brings him around the circle to "4," with whom he fights the second battle. Continuing in this manner, the order in which the warrior will fight his foes is 3, 4, 6, 2, 5, 7, 1.

Two Riders

58 miles. In an hour the first rider traveled 30 miles and the other 28 miles, so they were 58 miles apart one hour before they met each other.

Jousting Tournament Number

Sir Bale's number was 5. Four numbers are less than 5: 1, 2, 3, and 4. Six numbers are greater than 5: 6, 7, 8, 9, 10, 11. The product of 4 and 6 is 24. The answer would be the same if Sir Bale's number were 7; then there would be six numbers less than 7 and four numbers greater than 7.

Knights and Their Weapons

C. Only the knight and the weapon next to one another move—the knight up, the weapon down.

Medieval Merry-Go-Round

D. Black and white knights and ladies alternate as they spin counter-clockwise. Horse and dragon spin clockwise.

To the King's Castle

8 miles. Alf's answer to Beryl's first question was that the distance from their cottage to the point where she posed the question was three times the distance in miles from that point to the inn. Let x = the distance in miles from that point to the inn.

Alf's answer to Beryl's second question was that the distance to the castle from the point where she asked the second question was three times as far as the distance they had gone since leaving the inn. Let y = the distance in miles they had gone since leaving the inn. The distance between the points on the trip where the two questions were asked was 2 miles. The diagram below clarifies the puzzle.

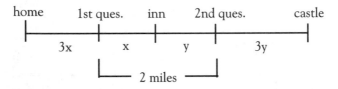

Since x + y = 2, it follows that 3(x + y) = 6. But 3 (x + y) is the same as 3x + 3y, distances that are marked in the diagram. The total distance, therefore, is (x + y) + (3x + 3y) miles, which is 2 + 6 = 8 miles.

How Many Handshakes?

105. The first knight shakes the hand of fourteen other knights. The second, having already shaken hands with the first, shakes the hand of thirteen others; the third, having shaken hands with the first and second, shakes hands with twelve others, and so forth. So we have the answer: 14 + 13 + 12 + 11 + 10 + 9 + 8 + 7 + 6 + 5 + 4 + 3 + 2 + 1 = 105.

Which Coin Is Lighter?

One way to accomplish the task is as follows. Peppi first divides the fifty coins into three groups: two of seventeen each and one of sixteen.

First Weighing: Peppi uses the scale to compare the two groups of seventeen. He places one group on one side of the scale and the other group on the other side. If one side is lighter than the other, the light coin has been identified as being in one particular group of seventeen coins. If the two sides balance, the light coin is in the group of sixteen that was not weighed.

Next, Peppi divides the group of sixteen coins, or the group of seventeen coins, whichever has been determined to contain the lighter coin, into three groups. If there are sixteen coins, he divides them into two groups of five coins each and one group of six coins. If there are seventeen coins, he divides them into two groups of six coins each and one group of five coins.

Second Weighing: Following the method outlined above Peppi identifies which one of the three groups contains the lighter coin. In other words, he balances the two groups of five coins against each other or the two groups of six coins against each other, depending on the result of the first weighing.

The second weighing identifies a group of either five or six coins that contains the lighter coin. If the light coin is in the former group, Peppi divides the five coins into two groups of two each, leaving one coin by itself. If it is the latter group, he divides the six coins into three groups of two each.

Third Weighing: Peppi compares two groups that have two coins each. If they balance on the scale, and only one coin remains in the third group, then the coin in the third group is the light one. If they don't balance, then the light coin is in the lighter group of two coins. If they do balance, the remaining group of two coins contains the lighter coin.

Fourth Weighing: If necessary, Peppi compares two single coins against each other to identify the light coin.

What Day of the Week Is It? I

Sunday. If it were Tuesday, Thursday, or Saturday, days on which the inhabitant always tells the truth, he would not lie and say he had told the truth on the previous day. If it were Monday, Wednesday, or Friday, days on which he always lies, he would not say he had told the truth on the previous day—for such a statement would be true. It is Sunday, a day on which the inhabitant tells the truth, and the only day of the week on which it is true that he tells the truth on the preceding day.

Minotaur Fighters

Logi had 78, Magnus had 42, Nepo had 24. The best way to solve this problem is by making a table that begins at the end of the lending:

Logi		Magnus		Nepo	
48	+	48	+	48	= 144
↓		↓		↓	
24	+	24	+	96	= 144
↓		↓		↓	
12	+	84	+	48	= 144
↓		↓		↓	
72	+	42	+	24	= 144

A Princess or a Dragon? II

The middle cave does not contain a princess, since its sign says it contains a dragon, and the cave containing the princess has a true statement on its sign. Also, if the middle cave contained a dragon, it would not say so, since only the sign on the cave with the princess has a true statement on it. Thus, the middle cave is empty. So, the sign on the middle cave is false. Since the middle cave is empty, the sign on cave C bears a true statement on it. So it contains the princess. The sign above cave A, is, by elimination, false and must contain the dragon.

Genie Hijinks

C. The foods spin counterclockwise around animals.

Anti-Ogre Potions

Seven. If the wizard took out four potions, he certainly would have two of the same kind, but not necessarily the ogre-fighters. He could have two of the evil wizard-vanquishers or the dragon-destroyers. And what good would they be in combat with an ogre?

If he took out five potions, he might wind up with three dragon-destroyers, two evil wizard-vanquishers, and no ogre-fighters. If he grabbed for six potions, they might include three dragon-destroyers, two wizard-vanquishers, and one ogre-fighter. But if he took out seven, he would have to have at least two ogre-fighters, since only five other potions were not ogre-fighters.

King Arthur Meets with King Balfour

576 ways. Without loss of generality, choose the knight for seat #2 first. From what we are told, he must be a knight of King Balfour. He can be chosen in four different ways. Next, choose the knight for seat #3. He is a knight of King Arthur, and he too can be chosen in four different ways. Then, seat #4 can be filled in three ways, from among Balfour's remaining three knights. Similarly, seats 7 and 8 can be filled in two ways each, and seats 9 and 10 in two ways each. So the required computation is: $4 \times 4 \times 3 \times 3 \times 2 \times 2 \times 1 \times 1$, which equals 576.

Genie Horseplay

B. The horse immediately to the left of the genie grows. The horse to the immediate right of the genie shrinks.

Did the Dragon Catch Pryor?

No, Pryor made it to the sea cave with less than four seconds to spare. If Wivere were to catch up with Pryor, he had to cover 7 miles before Pryor covered 2 miles. Pryor ran at a constant rate of 20 miles per hour, so he covered 2 miles in 6 minutes. As for Wivere, he ran the first mile in 3 minutes, the second in 1.5 minutes, the third in 0.75 minutes, the fourth in 0.375 minutes, the fifth in 0.1875 minutes, the sixth in 0.09375 minutes, and the seventh in 0.046875 minutes. Thus, Wivere needed 5.953125 minutes to run 7 miles. Add to this time the 6 seconds (0.1 minutes) he hesitated and Wivere reached the sea in 6.053125 minutes, or 6 minutes and about 3.4 seconds.

We can only hope that Pryor wasn't harmed by Wivere's fiery breath!

About the Authors

Born near Richmond, Virginia, **Margaret Edmiston** received her A.B. from Upsala College, studied graduate psychology at Columbia University, and later received her M.A. in mathematics from West Georgia College. Following a long career in consumer marketing research, she now pursues writing, puzzle-making, and teaching mathematics. A longtime contributor to puzzle magazines under the names Margaret Edmiston, Margaret Shoop and Sarah Brighton, among others, she has a continuing interest in writing for children and finds special joy and fulfillment in teaching mathematics as a member of the adjunct faculty of Virginia Commonwealth University.

Ms. Edmiston lives in Chesterfield County, near Richmond.

Muriel Mandell is the author of a dozen books for children, the latest of which was *Simple Experiments in Time*. She has been a Washington correspondent, a police reporter, a columnist, and a magazine editor. She has taught in New York City at all levels from kindergarten to graduate school and developed and coordinated a program for the improvement of writing which was validated by New York State for replication. She now uses her logic skills teaching computer programs to seniors—and coping with two adult sons and a granddaughter.

Index

Page key: puzzle, *clue*, **solution**

127